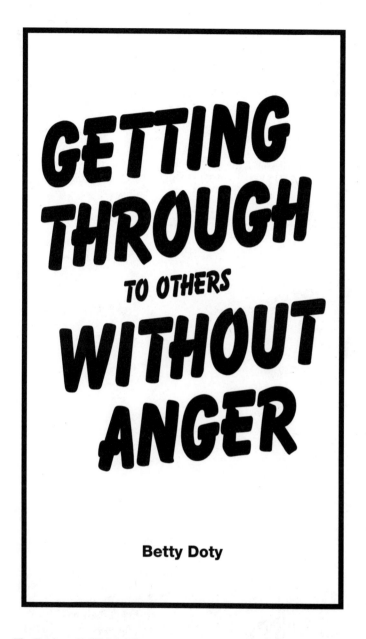

GETTING THROUGH

TO OTHERS

WITHOUT ANGER

Betty Doty

The Bookery Publishing Company – 6899 Riata Dr., Redding, CA96002

Books by Betty Doty and Pat Rooney –
 SHAKE THE ANGER HABIT!
 THE ANGER PUZZLE

Book by Betty Doty and Rebecca Meredith –
 HEY LOOK… I MADE A BOOK!

Books by Betty Doty –
 BREAK THE ANGER TRAP
 MARRIAGE INSURANCE
 PUBLISH YOUR OWN HANDBOUND BOOKS

Audio Cassette –
 SHAKE THE ANGER HABIT!

acid-free recycled paper

First printing 1993

Table of Contents

Part I

Chapter

  1   Entering the counseling room 1
  2   Comments on my response to come 5
  3   Shifting sand 7
  4   Wetting down the sand 11
  5   Wanting help 13
  6   Fighting to get help 17
  7   The headband 19
  8   One starting place for problem solving 23
  9   A better starting place 25
 10   Balancing is lonely.....................................27
 11   Guessing at others' motivations, #1 31
 12   Guessing at others' motivations, #2 33
 13   A garbage heap 35
 14   Not helping each other directly 37
 15   Making up theories for safety 41
 16   A theory that works 45
 17   It's a choice..49
 18   A wrong turn 51
 19   Above the parade 55
 20   "I've tried everything" 57
 21   Niceness won't work 59
 22   Anger and niceness 63
 23   The problem isn't the hair in the soup 67
 24   Observing or judging 71
 25   Expecting too much of wild cards 73
 26   Taking things personally 77
 27   Acceptance and appreciation 83

Table of Contents
(continued)

28	Not crazy?	87
29	We can't listen if …	89
30	Hearing feelings	93
31	Getting through to each other	97
32	The anger trap	101
33	Closing the first counseling session	117

Part II

34	Follow-up session, comments and questions	119
35	What if we can't choose to believe?	123
36	Others' anger	127
37	A couple's experience	133
38	Quiz for readers	137
39	One man's experience	141
40	A common power struggle with couples	149
41	Implications for society	157

Supplement #1 Some suggestions for getting through without anger ... 164

Supplement #2 Some questions asked at seminars and workshops ... 168

Supplement #3 A Road Map ... 171

Supplement #4 Comments on angry pleasers (those controlled by fear of others' anger) ... 178

Bibliography ... 209
Index ... 213
Order form ... 214

Foreword

Power struggles, "bad guys," winners and losers and the dreary saga of anger loosed into a fragile world. These are the targets of Betty Doty and she doesn't waver and she doesn't blink. We need her insights now more than ever.

In this book, as in her previous books, Doty tries to **get through** to us that there is a way to enhance our understanding of human discord, to mend the unhappy rifts with our family and fellows, and to avoid the further collection of failed expectations, grievances and grudges. This way is both clear-headed and compassionate... and available **right now** to **everybody**.

It will come as no surprise to others in the people-helping business that healing may well begin with just one person's learning how to let the other feel deeply heard...and accepted...as is. That's when profound changes follow.

We can be delivered, for example, from self-righteousness, and **they** can stop feeling blamed. That's when **we** can begin to really talk **with** each other. Talking **with** is all we've got, folks, and it's all we need.

Carol A. Fleming, Ph.D.
San Francisco, CA

Chapter 1

Entering the counseling room

"I've tried everything...nothing works... I'm at the end of my rope... there's nowhere to turn..."

Nearly every day I hear these words in the family counseling room. What can I do? Is there a certain "something" I can pass on to each person, a "something" which can be used to reverse this pattern?

If so, does this same "something" fit each person who comes in for counseling?

As far as I can tell, the answer well may be **yes.** I think there really is a "something" which fits each person. **But I want to invite you inside the counseling room (by way of this book) so you** can see it ... and check it out for your-self.

Maybe you can imagine deciding to make an appointment here to talk over a problem. If so, here's an easy way to see if this "something" would fit you. **Stop reading at the end of this chapter and imagine what you'd be telling me if you were actually here.**

To make your imagining easier, it will help you to know you're beginning a three-hour session. And maybe you can visualize being in a quiet, comfortable room, and there's lush greenery outside a large window.

While you're settling in, I'd say some-thing like this, "Just tell me what you want me to know."

Even though most people hesitate at first, they usually talk for an hour or two, and I'd expect you to do the same. (I purposely keep my head buried in my notebook to avoid giving you any feedback at all. I want to hear what **you** want to say, completely uninfluenced by me.)

After an hour or so, when you're tying up loose ends, I'd ask you to let me know when you're ready to hear my response.

By the time you'd be ready to listen, we'd probably take a short break. Maybe I'd joke a little about getting equal time, and we'd probably relax a few minutes before going on.

Here's the place to stop reading if you want to imagine what you'd tell me ... before hearing my response. Remember that I won't interrupt, and you'll just tell me what you want me to know. (Or maybe you'll stop here and write out your problem instead. And for the fun of it, maybe you'll make some notes on what you expect me to say.)

Chapter 2

Comments on my response to come

It's true that even though I present the same basics to each person, I'll probably emphasize different points. But no one misses getting the whole package.

Sometimes I take more by-ways than others, and sometimes I do a fast summary. (The short version is needed when the person has just talked, non-stop, for three hours.) Because I'm writing now instead of talking, you'll get the long version...plus some additions.

❧

Probably my first feedback will be to show that I've truly heard each person's desperation, the desperation of knowing that whatever they're doing isn't working. (Speakers sometimes take very long detours before they're able to say this clearly.)

Since I think the best problem solving starts with the best description of what's actually happening, my response is composed of my guesses about what seems to be going on. These guesses are based on thousands of hours of listening, and mostly I'm reporting to each person what I've learned.

As I'm talking, I'll keep giving out reminders **that the only thing I'm truly an expert on is my own opinion:** "From what I can tell...It's my guess...the way it seems to me..."

Usually, after I've listened so long to each person, I'm impressed that they have such an enormous number of pieces of whatever puzzle they're trying to solve. But the "I've-tried-everything" talk indicates that their pieces obviously aren't fitting together the way they'd like. **When I tell each person that it's my guess that only a little fine-tuning is needed, they're usually surprised. Evidently it's just too hard to believe, at first, that it's possible to merely rearrange the pieces of their own puzzle (and maybe add a few tiny new ones)...and things can get better fast.**

Chapter 3

Shifting sand

As I see it, when we say, "I've tried everything," we're trapped in some kind of power struggle. And the trap snaps shut when we're sure we know the way things ought to be.

Let's take a broader view and see where it leads.

Maybe we're in a world in which we're all like shifting sand. Not only are we able to move in any direction at any time, but we seem to be doing just that. I look at someone, turn my head, then look back and they've changed.

(Living in such a world might be somewhat like trying to work a jigsaw puzzle in which each piece is constantly changing.)

It's using the image of all of us walking in shifting sand which helps to see that our first priority is just learning to keep balanced physically.

Not only this takes great concentration and keen observation of the laws of nature, but it also requires that we "hold up our heads." And we equate this with feeling good about ourselves.

But how do we know we deserve to hold up our heads? Our self-doubts can be nearly overwhelming. After all, how do we know we're "worth our salt?"...and "up to snuff?" **What is it we can tell ourselves** so we can believe that we're all right the way we are... in spite of obvious limitations?

I see us as consciously or unconsciously working to keep our balance, **all the time asking ourselves innumerable questions:** Shall I move my arm here? scratch my nose? wash my hands? put on a coat? talk to my boss? take a pill? run around the block? eat a cracker? play with the kittens? call my mom? think about Jack?

Seems to me the essence of all this is just one question: What is it I can do to keep my balance in shifting sand...**with what I've got this exact second?**

If we're unable to ask this crucial question, we stay in a pattern of believing that whatever we have, **at this second,** isn't enough. So we stay determined to try harder than ever **to get what we think is missing.**

Chapter 4

Wetting down the sand

The trouble which leads to a counseling room, as far as I can tell, comes from defining our problems this way: We believe we absolutely cannot feel good (balanced, with heads up) **unless we wet down the shifting sand and get it to stay the way we think it ought to be.**

Once we believe that's what we have to do, we stay off balance. We're busy leaning over, plotting, pushing, shoving, molding and holding. But the sand just isn't co-operating. When we try harder and oftener, we stumble more and fail more. Because we're off balance, we're probably bruising everything we touch. Instead of getting the good feelings we keep expecting, we're provoking **more** resistance and **more** retaliation.

At first when we fail, our conclusion usually is that we just haven't tried hard enough…yet.

But what happens when we're absolutely convinced we've tried everything? What conclusion can we reach except that others aren't helping us enough? Isn't it obvious that they're responsible for our failures?

My experience is that people in the counseling room have been spending an enormous amount of their time trying to understand what's wrong. It's as if they're frantically trying to identify villains so they'll know who or what to "shape up."

For all of us, I think we **eventually** find that no matter who or what we believe to be at fault for our problems, and how much blaming and "shaping up" we can do, **we don't have the power to make that shifting-sand world the way we think it ought to be.**

Chapter 5

Wanting help

What's wrong with struggling to get what we think we ought to be able to get? Doesn't everybody do that?

I'm talking about the power struggles which come from believing that we absolutely have to reach one particular goal.

Once a goal becomes **too** important, there undoubtedly will be times that we'll try to reach it at others' expense. And every time we do so we hurt ourselves.

As far as I can tell, what we're so determined to get from others is their help. We become convinced that such help and cooperation is essential to reaching the goal of feeling good about ourselves.

The help we want may be direct or maybe we only want others **to avoid interfering with our balancing efforts.** But we desperately want that cooperation. If we're successful in getting it, we're likely to interpret our success as evidence of others' caring. So we want it, we want it, we want it.

But the more pushy we are for cooperation, **the more we overdo it and trigger resistance.** In our confusion, we may sadly say to ourselves, "If only they'd cooperate willingly, I wouldn't have to be so obnoxious."

When we're confused and disappointed that others aren't reacting in the way we expect, at some point we probably develop a kind of tunnel vision. It's as if our total focus is now on **others and their resistance.** By labeling that resistance badness, it's easy to conclude that such badness deserves punishment.

But hard as we try, it's impossible to do enough punishing to get what we really want, willingly-given cooperation.

When the good feelings we're seeking stay out of reach, we're locked in a series of power struggles. **We can see no alternative to fighting again and again for what we believe is essential.**

Let's look at power struggles in general. I think they're traps, as they can't end. By definition, they're composed of winners and losers. And when we're losers, the way we tolerate the pain is by planning to deliver a "knock-out blow" so we can "turn the tables." Surely, then, the fighting will cease and the villains will be "put in their place"... and we'll be established as winners, **once and for all.**

How discouraging it is to find that bigger blows lead only to bigger responses. And to make matters worse, because our lives are more and more consumed by the bigger blows and bigger responses, our real problems sit untended on the sidelines, unresolved and ever more threatening.

But what can we do? It's too painful to accept that we can't get what we think we ought to be able to get. So we have to keep on fighting, don't we?

Chapter 6

Fighting to get help

Why would any of us stay in power struggles, futilely trying to make shifting sand the way it ought to be?

I think we stay trapped in such a pattern (whether our power struggles are with others or within ourselves) **only** because we truly don't know an alternative.

From what I can tell, what keeps us stuck is believing that we have **only** two choices, to fight or give up. ("I can't let 'em walk all over me, can I?...I'd rather be dead than give up.")

From this position we stay blinded to these two possibilities: **What if it's the way we define our problems** (what we think we ought to be able to get from shifting sand) **which causes our dilemma?**

And what if our failures are because we're trying to do something impossible, something such as getting a decisive win from inside a power struggle?

Let's look at what happens when we stay stuck in a fight-or-give-up mindset.

Chapter 7

The headband

I think this true story illustrates the irrational desperation of a far-advanced power struggle.

A junior high school student was fighting with the principal over the school dress code, and the battle eventually settled on the girl's wearing a headband. As you can guess, the intensity of each person's back-and-forth moves increased as both were finding they couldn't get a decisive win.

> **Principal:** "I can't give up...
> I've got to show these
> kids who's boss or
> they'd run all over
> me..."

Girl: "You should see what that guy's been doing … I've got to show him he can't do that to me and get away with it."

One night, when the girl got home from school, she took out a needle and thread... and she sewed her headband to her forehead.

Surely, it would have seemed that the principal might have backed off at that point, maybe mumbling, "...crazy kid...she's gonna' kill herself..."

When I asked the girl what happened next, she told me that the principal hadn't backed off at all, but instead just kept hassling her.

I think her response gives a fascinating glimpse inside a power struggle. It didn't occur to the girl to say, "We **both** kept hassling each other."

At seminars here, we sometimes discuss this true story. It's interesting to me to see that the early discussion usually consists of exchanging judgments about who's right and who's wrong. This is followed by each person's best theories about how either the principal or the girl might have gotten a decisive win.

Since it's my belief that there are no decisive wins possible inside a power struggle, what I see is that two individuals can get caught up in a power-struggle trap...and they can't find their way out.

In the counseling room, when I see people with this kind of a mindset, my guess is that they're **continually** engrossed in **countless** power struggles. It's likely that they habitually see everyone in terms of friends or enemies, winners or losers, wrong or right. **And it takes real vigilance to search out and punish those "bad guys," the ones trying to get the best of them...the ones thwarting their best efforts to be a winner.**

For those with the habit of seeing the world from this point of view, I suspect that right this minute, wherever they are, they're seeking out individuals with a mindset similar to theirs.

If you listen closely, maybe you can hear someone saying these fateful words: **"But I couldn't let 'em get away with it, could I?... over my dead body..."**

Sometimes I call a power-struggle mindset an anger trap...or an anger habit. Whatever label we use, let's see what kind of thinking it takes to replace it with something which works better.

Chapter 8

One starting place for problem solving

One way of thinking about the world is to visualize all of us walking in a parade going from birth to death. This image helps us see how important it is to keep upright and moving. And it also shows that survival will depend on learning how to get up fast after each fall.

What is it that determines whether we'll get up fast?...get up slowly?...or not at all?

I think the key is our **starting position** for problem solving. Let's pose a problem and look at it from two different starting positions. Here's the problem.

We'll say we're working on a project (maybe a puzzle of some kind) and we want ten pieces...but we've only got two.

One way of approaching the problem stems from the belief that the **only** way we can move ahead is by getting the **missing pieces.** Let's see what happens.

Because we aren't moving, everyone in the parade is running into us. We're less and less able to function as we're increasingly reeling from repeated blows and confusion.

Because we're losing our balance more often, we're also discouraged and less willing to hold up our heads.

From this **starting position** for problem solving, our failures are inevitable. And each failure hurts more than the last.

It's when the hurting becomes unbearable that we have no choice but to stay down, full time. We're totally unable to risk the pain of more failure.

Then the parade is not only passing us by, but we're being trampled.

With the utmost effort, maybe we can do one more thing: We can shake our fists at the "bad guys" who are leaving us stranded.

Chapter 9

A better starting place

Let's look at another **starting place** for working on the same project **(for which we've got two pieces when we wanted ten).**

We can focus on what we've got... **instead of the opposite.**

This means that whatever problems we're trying to solve, we start in the same place with the same question: **What is it I can do with what I've got...this second?**

By reminding ourselves of this question, we stay alert and looking ahead. We're habitually better able to handle whatever comes ... at each second.

Maybe you'll notice that from this starting position, it wouldn't matter how many pieces of the problem we'd be dealing with, as the starting **question**, the starting **position,** would still be the same. **What is it I can do with what I've got...this second?**

It's true that this kind of thinking calls for "fast footwork" if we really want to keep "landing on our feet." And of course "fast footwork" is risky, especially in shifting sand.

But trying to avoid the risks is even worse. We'd stay stuck in power struggles, incessantly fighting to "lay the groundwork" so we can walk solidly in the shifting sand.

❧

Fortunately, learning fast footwork can become fun. At some point, that fun leads to more and more pride and self-confidence.

Chapter 10

Balancing is lonely

When we look more closely at the problem of keeping balanced, one thing is clear: **It's lonely.**

We can see this by watching a baby learning to walk.

No amount of coaching from the sidelines can change the fact that keeping balanced is something each of us has to do for ourselves. And each step, always, is risky.

Maybe one of the worst pitfalls is "looking like a fool." Yet we aren't made so we can ever be absolutely sure, in advance, if any step is right for us. Certainly it's a common experience to plan something and believe we know exactly where to step... **yet later find how wrong we were.**

If we ourselves can't know, for sure, what's right for us until we actually take any step, **it's clear to me that those on the sidelines also can't know for sure, and in advance.**

When we're scared and teetering, can we talk to each other for comfort? Only somewhat. It's just too complicated. We can't really tell others about the decisions we're making, every second, about what we're doing to keep balanced.

If we try to tell others, there's too much to tell. And they usually can't listen much (even if they want to), as they're too busy making decisions about their own balance.

Our thoughts come too fast for words, anyway, so we can never say enough. And the words aren't available. If I say, "I hurt," for example, I can't make you understand exactly how I hurt, how much, how often, or how important the hurt is to me. Besides that, the hurt is probably changing as I'm talking.

We'll say a teenage boy has just wrecked his father's car on a Saturday night. And the boy is desperately trying to explain to his father what happened (maybe the details of what problem he was trying to solve at the second of the crash): "Joe said this...and Pete said that...and I thought maybe..."

It's not much of a surprise that many a father would give up trying to understand. And he'd break in with something like this: "You stupid kid..."

Chapter 11

Guessing at others' motivations, #1

What happens if we actually believe we have the power to know what's going on with another?

Here's an example of how wrong we can be.

A woman told me that in the past, when she'd feel depressed, she'd call her best friend to come over and sit with her. In spite of her pleading, the friend would never come, saying instead, "Come on over to my place."

Each time this happened, the depressed woman would very reluctantly get up out of bed, get dressed and go across town to her friend's. When she'd get there, she'd be more depressed and resentful as she couldn't see why the friend hadn't come her way (as it was obvious the friend was just puttering around and not doing anything important).

The depressed woman was certain that if her friend really cared for her she'd have come over when begged to do so. Convinced that her friend was no real friend, she pulled away, and the friendship was never the same.

Years later, the woman who had been depressed in the past, finally told the friend why she'd been angry with her all these years.

The friend's response (and this is a true story) was this: "When you asked me to come I was having trouble with my knees...and I didn't want anybody to know about it. I just couldn't walk up your steps."

Chapter 12

Guessing at others' motivations ,#2

Here's another story to show that our guesses about what's going on aren't as accurate as we'd like to believe.

A man has just bought a new car, and it's red and shining. He's driving it out of the showroom and he can hardly contain his pride. As he's getting close to home, he's going through a road-cut. And he suddenly hears rocks hitting the top of his car.

Immediately he's in a rage, and he jerks the car to a halt...jumps out...and starts running up the hill. He's completely ready to strangle those kids who would dare throw rocks on his precious beauty.

As he's running up the hill, he sees a little boy (maybe 6 or 7 years old). And the boy is running toward him, and he's crying. He's saying, "Mister, mister, I hated to do that... but my little sister fell down on her face and I'm afraid she's dead."

Chapter 13

A garbage heap

I suspect that our guesses about each other's motives are **usually** wrong. That's because I see our brain as a garbage heap, and it's as if we're all frantically trying to keep from being overwhelmed with unsorted garbage. So we're **incessantly** rummaging around, making decisions about what to keep...or toss...or shift around.

Somewhere inside that lifetime collection of shifting tidbits, **I think there's a natural computer which is trying to help us keep balanced.** So we keep getting tiny messages: "Try this...try that ..."

Seems to me it would be completely impossible to be familiar with the components of another's garbage heap, much less know how they're arranged at any one second.

Truly understanding how another human being is keeping balanced seems as unlikely as a fish's understanding the desert.

... Or (and this may seem to be an extreme example), what if we're expecting to project an image of our whirling tidbits of garbage in exactly the right pattern so another mass of whirling garbage can perceive them at this exact second...and then respond, "Now I get the picture."

Chapter 14

Not helping each other directly

When we're living by guesses, and devoting our lives to trying to find out what others want so we can help them, what happens?

I think we'd find ourselves saying, many, many times, "But I was only trying to help ...that's no crime, is it?"

What I see is that our "help" can be intrusive and irritating to others and their garbage sorting. We may not realize that we not only can't use **our own garbage heap** to know exactly what **another** wants, at any one second, **but the other person usually can't even tell us.**

A person might be saying to you, for example, " I feel kind of shaky tonight...and I think I'd feel better if you'd..."

Whatever you'd do in response, the other could say, "But I still don't feel better... I wish you'd try something else..." So you might try something else. And the other could respond again, "No, no, I still don't feel better. Try that instead."

This could go on and on, and it probably will as long as you truly believe that if you'll try hard enough, you can make the other feel better... more balanced.

(I think this situation is especially confusing because we **do** have the power to distract each other from our problems...**at times**...and that can be somewhat helpful... **at times.**)

Of course we do truly help each other occasionally. And I suspect that it usually happens accidentally instead of by plan.

It's trying to help each other **directly**, and probably overdoing it, that I see as harmful. Would-be recipients of our "help" may feel confused and uncomfortable at having to push us away. And we're probably hurting others by robbing them of chances to gain confidence by doing things themselves.

Recipients of our "help" may sadly be asking themselves this question: "Why do I want to lash out at you when you're doing everything to help me?" And they probably give themselves this answer: "I must be the one who's bad, as obviously you're good. You're the one who's trying so hard to help me."

With so much confusion surrounding our helping efforts, it's no wonder that much of our time is spent defending ourselves and feeling hurt: "**Nobody knows how hard I try** ...No one will **ever** understand me...I was just trying to..."

Consider this question: **How many times, when you desperately needed help, could anyone give it to you in exactly the right way...and at exactly the right time...and the right place?**

What's fascinating about this, from my point of view, is the importance we usually attach to being able to **give** help directly as well as **get** help directly.

Chapter 15

Making up theories for safety

How do we find the courage to keep going when every step we take is into the unknown? And we can't really understand each other...or help or get much help from each other.

In the search for ways to be as comfortable as possible in such a world, we keep making up theories to live by. Maybe they fit belief systems with well-known labels, or maybe we create our own systems. But I see us as busy observing, making predictions and adjusting our theories all the time. "Live and learn," we say to each other.

But no matter how much we long to fully understand what's happening so we can feel more comfortable in a scary world, we're tremendously limited. For example, if it were possible for all the secrets of the universe to fly down out of the sky and land at our feet, I think this probably is what would happen: **Just because we're human,** we could only focus on a tiny portion of them …much less understand them.

How can we ever feel comfortable with our limitations? How can we feel adequate? that we're enough? able to keep from being overwhelmed? able to understand enough to find our way and get at least a little cooperation when the going is especially rough?

I'll comment briefly on just a few of our made-up theories.

⬜⬜⬜ **We can believe** that in order to be safe from criticism ("looking like a fool"), the fewer decisions we make the better. If we'll just tiptoe around and keep out of sight, we'll be all right.

If we use this theory to try to keep moving in a parade, I don't think we'd like the result. I suspect we'd be buffeted from all sides, maybe ending up on the sidelines, bruised and bleeding. Then we'd probably feel like an outcast...a "nobody."

❑❑❑ **We can believe** that we'll escape the feared criticism if we'll play Follow the Leader.

Walking in a parade, the price we'd pay would be our own help-lessness. If the leader is making all the decisions, how can we make things better when they go wrong? (No wonder we get so desperate for power to combat helplessness that we often use the easiest power to find: We blame the leaders.)

❑❑❑ **We can believe** that if we'll be nice and helpful enough, others will want to help us (as we're trying to do for them).

But walking in a parade, with all of us fighting for our own balance, it's unlikely, if not impossible, that we can know what each person wants and give it to them. More likely, we'll be saying: **"Those un-grateful wretches...they don't care if I work my fingers to the bone trying to help 'em."**

Chapter 16

A theory that works

Seems to me that our only safety lies in finding theories that help us do our own fast footwork. We know that the more we're able to "take things in stride," the more we'll enjoy what we're doing.

I'll lay out the theory I use which helps me with fast footwork.

As I wrote earlier, I'm suggesting that there's a natural computer inside my garbage heap, and it's helping me keep balanced. It's my choice to believe I'm made so that **I'm always doing the best I can,** just trying to keep balanced (with whatever combination of tidbits my computer is using at any one minute).

Since my garbage heap is enormously

complicated and mostly unconscious, I realize that I can't know exactly and completely why I'm doing what I'm doing at any one time.

Fortunately, I don't need to offer facts to show that I'm doing my best, as I'm not talking about facts. I'm talking about my **choice** to believe that whatever I do, **by my own description of the way I'm made,** is my best at this precise moment.

It's no crime to be human and be forced to make decisions with never enough information.

My belief that I'm doing the best I can goes with me wherever I go. Two years from now, or at any time, whatever I'm doing, **in advance** I'll choose to believe that I'll be doing the best I can…every second. It's as if I'm taking my judge and jury with me.

Because I choose this belief, I don't ever waste time in self-criticism, feeling guilty or being defensive. Whenever I fall down, I jump up and land on my feet, ready to try again. Because I'm moving in the parade, my starting position is such that I stay ready to handle whatever's coming next.

This is fascinating to me because the prevailing belief seems to be that self-criticism is the best way to push ourselves to new and greater goals. But it's my experience that a starting place of accepting ourselves as doing our best…this minute…makes **whatever we do** less stressful. And from that starting place, we're more and more effective.

Chapter 17

It's a choice

What I think is interesting is that someone had to tell me that I had a choice about feeling good about myself (about whether I'm doing my best or not). I thought that my feeling good or bad just happened. Doesn't everyone feel good when things are going good, and bad when they're not? Isn't that the way the world is made?

What I'm talking about is learning how to feel good about ourselves (the way we're keeping balanced) **all the time** no matter what's happening. And I see this as simply realizing that it's a matter of our own choice about what we believe.

What's important to me is that I've given up even trying to judge others. In order to judge them, I thought I had to be able to do the impossible: understand them first. Once

I could see that complete understanding was impossible, the judging disappeared.

This had a wonderful side benefit. Because I'm not judging, I'm not afraid of others' judgments of me. That's because I now know, from my own experience, that **everyone** isn't as judgmental as I used to be. And I can see that it was **my own** judgmentalness, projected on others, which was keeping me fearful in every move I made.

Chapter 18

A wrong turn

What happens if we choose to believe that we're **not** doing the best we can?

I think we make a serious wrong turn. It means we live in fear that we're actually "bad guys." These fears are expressed in a variety of ways, but what I hear most in the counseling room is this: "There must be something wrong with me...maybe there's a piece missing...or there's a monster buried inside... "

These fears vary in intensity from time to time, but they're persistent and can be terrifying. I suspect that whether we do it consciously or unconsciously, **many of us** are spending **much** of our time trying to show that we're really a "good guy." We want to make certain no one can ever suspect that there might possibly be a "bad guy" hidden inside.

If our primary life work is trying to prove we're a "good guy," we confuse ourselves and others by trying to prove what we don't need to prove.

Once we're on a losing course, repeatedly trying to prove what we don't need to prove, we reach further and oftener for those **"missing pieces"** (the evidence we think we need to prove we're not a "bad guy").

It's as if we think of the main parade as going along at street level, and for some reason, we're afraid we're actually six inches below. So we keep fighting to show we deserve to be at street level ... at the very least.

But the view from this down position is always distorted. For one thing, we see everyone in terms of up or down, above us or below us, winners or losers, big or little: "He's too high and mighty...gotta' take him down a peg or two..." We stay extremely busy, as it takes great vigilance to ferret out

every single person trying to "lord it over us."

As we're stumbling and lurching, always fighting to hold up our heads, we're making terrible decisions. It's no wonder that we find it so hard to pronounce ourselves as doing our best.

So we stay convinced that we just aren't the way we ought to be. And we won't be "up to snuff" unless we're better, taller, thinner, stronger, nicer...or whatever we think will prove our case.

Now we're in an unending power struggle to "show up" those people who won't appreciate us and help us so we can look like "good guys." Yet they rarely cooperate willingly. In fact, they probably refuse to acknowledge that we're better, taller, thinner, stronger, nicer.

But constantly trying to show up others carries a high price. The world inevitably becomes more hostile when we're constantly thinking...and acting...on this belief: "I've got to get 'em before they get me."

I don't think we can break out of this pattern until we realize that we can **choose** to believe that we're already doing our best and **we don't need any kind of facts and comparisons with others to prove it.**

Chapter 19

Above the parade

Maybe we can imagine walking in a parade, and we'll say we've drawn a line parallel to the parade, but above our heads. We've decided that we need to get to some point so we can walk that imaginary line up in the sky. Then nobody will suspect that we really belong six inches below the parade.

However we describe our quest, we say to ourselves: "**If only** I can reach that spot up there I'll find what I'm seeking. **Then** I'll feel better, and **then** I'll get the acceptance, appreciation, cooperation and caring I deserve."

What I see in this is an over-reach/fall-back pattern. We stay whirling around up above the parade, relentlessly searching in a kind of no-man's land. It doesn't feel good because we started from a down position.

So we take our not-really-all-right feelings with us wherever we go. Nothing we find helps us feel better... **about ourselves.**

What a difference a starting place makes. When we assume that we're all on equal footing and belong in the same parade, we're not looking to be either up or down. We see that we're **all** struggling and stumbling...**all** forced to do fast footwork ... and **all uneasy with it at times.**

Chapter 20

"I've tried everything"

As we're flying around up in the sky, trying to avoid falling down into that shifting sand, or falling even lower, at some point we reach this conclusion: The reason we can't stay up in the sky (where we think we ought to be) is that others aren't helping us enough. So we have to try harder than ever to convince them that we deserve help. After all, look how hard we're trying.

Since our failures are guaranteed **(as the help we keep expecting is for what we have to do for ourselves, keep our own balance in the parade)**, it might seem that the ways we try to get help wouldn't matter.

But here's the problem. **From an off-balance position, the two most common ways we use to make things better actually** increase the pain for both ourselves and others.

Here are the two methods: **First we try to be nice enough that we'll deserve help. And if that fails, we get mad and pushy.**

In the counseling room I often hear these sad words: "But I tried being nice…" It's as if the speaker had no alternative but to throw a fit when another person wouldn't co-operate.

What I see, is that whether we're trying to get what we want either by niceness or the opposite, others eventually choose to stay away from us. They want out of range of our attempts to control them.

Seems to me we've trapped ourselves by believing that others should do the im-possible, **help us reach a goal that only we can reach (keep our own balance).** And we're making things worse by trying to sway them to seeing things our way… and gettting mad because they won't be swayed.

Chapter 21

Niceness won't work

In the counseling room, when I see people in power struggles trying to get help and cooperation, the terror which brings them in is this: They've found that their niceness won't work.

They sadly say, **"Nothing I ever did was good enough...I couldn't please 'em no matter what I did."**

It's as if they're pronouncing themselves as complete failures in their life work. **("...and nobody knows how hard I try.")**

The way I see it, **we can't be nice enough that others will choose to lean over very long (and maybe lose their balance) in an effort to help us keep ours.**

When we can't be nice enough to get the help we want, that's when we conclude that anger is justified. After all, don't we deserve help because we're doing so much for others? **Oh, the excruciating anguish of knowing that they won't help us when we need it.**

We suffer in silence as long as we can, but when we eventually explode, we feel guilty and things get worse. Our own ever-present fear of ourselves as a "bad guy" is reinforced. **"I'm just not that kind of person," we protest. "I don't know what got into me."**

Now we're certain there's a sinister pool of poison inside us, ready to spurt out whenever our back is turned. So we have to be on guard, full time, to hold that poison inside so we won't be exposed as a "bad guy."

We try **so hard** to be a "good guy," it's bad enough that we aren't appreciated. But it's just too much when others actually get angry at us. When our too-painful fears of our own "badness" come too close to the surface, we think we absolutely have to go on the attack in order to defend ourselves.

It's as if we think we see a mad dog bent on destroying us (exposing more of our own pain than we can handle), so we don't need to be too careful about what kind of rocks we throw.

Because ugly, futile power struggles follow, it's totally impossible to banish our fears of "badness." We can't feel good when we're violently attacking others and defending ourselves from their attacks.

And no matter how bloody the fight, we don't get the results we want: decisive proof that the other is the "bad" one, **at least worse and more wrong than we are** (so we can feel at least a little better ourselves).

Chapter 22

Anger and niceness

There's an interesting relationship between niceness and anger. I've come to believe that anger **primarily** comes from our disappointment that we can't please others (so we can get their help and cooperation... so we can look like "good guys").

I reach this conclusion from talking to the angriest people possible, some of whom want to see the entire world destroyed. (I also talk to those not quite so angry. They don't want see the entire world destroyed, just the people in it.)

But no matter who I'm talking with in the counseling room, I can hear their disappointment that they aren't pleasing someone. And they react in anger.

As I've written earlier, neither niceness nor anger will work to get those grains of shifting sand to be cooperative more than temporarily.

Getting angry because our niceness fails to get us **more** help and cooperation makes everything worse. I think the targets rightly perceive that we're trying to control them.

It's obvious that our controlling attempts are more apparent when we use anger instead of niceness. But with anger, either our targets fight back...or maybe they "walk on eggs" until they can get away from us. Now our worst fears are realized. We must really be bad. Whether others choose to fight back or tiptoe away, we're eventually left standing alone.

When the pain of our failures and the increasing isolation become too great to bear, we try to find painkillers. Alcohol and drugs, maybe, or suicide. Some people go into a fantasy world, and others just turn off their feelings and get numb.

Maybe the most common way of trying to get relief from pain is by blaming others.

Even though the initial blaming (triggering countless power struggles to expose others' "badness") can't really make us look better, the power struggles have one sure benefit. When we're absolutely desperate for a pain-free breath, we can "put the heat" on others so all eyes will be turned away from us...if only for a fraction of a second. At last...we can breathe.

Of course such blaming boomerangs. But if we're hurting enough, whatever ugliness follows, the blaming is worth that tiny respite we can get from our intolerable pain.

As I write this, the person who just left the counseling room had intense chest pains. Like so many others, he's been certain he's a "bad guy" for so long that his pain is nearly unendurable. (He knows he disappointed his mother.) His pain is literally that he's afraid to breathe. As bad as he thinks he is, just being alive means that he thinks he's probably hurting somebody.

Chapter 23

The problem isn't the hair in the soup

It's interesting to me that in our society our talk about anger focuses on the triggers for it. "OhTom, he always gets mad when... and Dick, he'll never blow up until..."

What if forming anger is merely a habit, and it comes from a habitual way of processing information so we believe we're justified in getting angry?

Seems to me that we've focused so long on the triggers for anger, and how bad it is to hold it inside, that we've missed something more important. **What if the problem is forming anger in the first place?**

In workshops here, we present a pantomime entitled "The Problem Isn't the Hair in the Soup."

Four men enter a restaurant separately, and each finds a hair in his soup.

The first man uses the hair to get some attention and have a little fun. He compares the hair with that of the waitress and kids her a little. Then he coils the hair around his finger and walks out...putting that precious hair in his shirt pocket, close to his heart.

The second man gets angry when he finds the hair, dumps the bowl of soup on the floor and stomps out.

The third man gets nauseated and runs for the door.

The fourth man (maybe the hungriest of them all) simply flips the hair out and slurps down the rest of the soup in one gulp.

For the workshop discussion which follows, this is the question: **If the angry**

man's problem wasn't the hair in the soup, what was it?

Many people say it's the man's attitude. And all agree that it came from something he brought with him into the restaurant. Some suggest that he may have had a fight with his wife earlier...or they'll offer other guesses about the triggers for his outburst.

From my point of view, the man has the anger habit. The way he sees the world keeps him convinced that he ought to be angry when things aren't the way he thinks they ought to be. Incessantly and automatically he justifies his anger.

(One confusing thing about anger is that temporarily it seems to work. We might swat a kid, for example, and get instant obedience. **But if that's the only problem-solving method we know, our worst fears about our "badness" will be reinforced, again and again. In the long run, we'll stand alone... again and again.)**

One thing to come out of discussions of the pantomime is that workshop participants are identifying with the man who got angry...and how horrible he must have felt soon after. We all agree that if the people from the restaurant later saw him on the street, they'd probably stay away from him, far away.

What also comes out of the discussion is how to break the anger habit. And we talk about replacing it with a habit which works better.

Maybe you remember the first man who found a hair in his soup, and that he used it to have some fun. (As he left the restaurant he was putting the hair in his shirt pocket close to his heart.) It seems likely that the man's lifelong habit is to **make the best of whatever comes...and enjoy it if he can.**

If this is his habitual starting position for problem solving, what would be the result?

I think we can safely guess that people aren't staying away from him to avoid his anger.

Chapter 24

Observing or judging

Here's one way of comparing two different starting places for problem solving: **observing** and **judging.**

Starting place #1, Observing: In the parade we're making the best possible observations of what's going on ahead of us. We learn to recognize hot water...and briar bushes. At the same time we're making sure we keep our heads up, our eyes forward and our feet on the ground. We're remembering, constantly, that our **best observations** are needed for our **best balancing decisions.** And we're staying busy making the best of whatever we've got... every second.

Starting place #2, Judging whether we're getting the help we believe we deserve: Because we haven't focused on our own fast footwork, we're focusing instead on trying to get the help we're incessantly trying to deserve, the help we believe we absolutely have to have. And judging our success is a full time job. Everything comes under intense scrutiny, maybe a moved eyebrow or a twitched lip. It's a desperate search for answers to our perpetual questions: "Am I going to get what I deserve?... Why not?...What am I doing wrong?... Will this help me or not?...Did that mean?... Will I deserve more help if I do this instead of that?... Shall I stand here?...or there?...or sit down instead?"

Let's look again at the two different starting places for problem solving. We'll say that we're detectives, and you and I are working on the same mystery. You're working from a list of your most accurate **observations.** And I'm working from a list of my best **judgments of what I think I deserve.** Which of us is most likely to solve the mystery?

Chapter 25

Expecting too much of wild cards

When I'm trying to describe life in the parade, I think of this image. Suppose the Game of Life is like a game of cards. We'd all be wild cards, the kind that can move in any direction and play anywhere. (Of course, there's really no card game played with all wild cards, but that's the way life is.)

Here's what I'm suggesting by using the image of us as playing cards moving in a parade: We'd all be standing up on end, and our balance would be very, very fragile.

It's obvious that only a little push would be enough to put us off balance at times. ("They just rub me the wrong way...")

I don't think we can look at each other and be able to know how much energy each person needs to keep balanced at any one time. So we can't tell if others have surplus energy to be shared.

I think we hurt each other, continually, by expecting too much help. For example, if I expect more help from you than I get, both of us might be hurt: I might be disappointed and you might feel inadequate.

What's confusing is that we have innumerable ways to hide from each other that our balance is slipping. So we usually judge by what we see, and that means constantly misinterpreting each other's motives: "She could have helped me with that...She wasn't doing anything...She doesn't care how hard I work...She'd do anything to hurt me..."

Someone is sure to ask, "But is it too much to ask that...?"

No matter what follows the "that," my answer is always **yes.** If we're expecting **what we aren't getting,** nothing can change the fact that the wild cards aren't lined up the way we want them to be...at this minute.

But someone may ask, "But what I want is so little…**Why can't they just help me a little?**" We don't need to know why we aren't getting the help we want. What I see is that it's always our choice to be hurt and angry, or not, if the wild cards aren't behaving the way we want them to.

How do we ever know how much to expect of ourselves and others? My answer is that we can look, this minute, to see what we're getting. That tells us what we can expect, this minute.

How do we get along…with what we can get…**willingly given**…at any one second? I think we all have to figure that out for ourselves.

We have to learn **from our own experience,** what makes fast footwork easier when the going gets rough. For example, we know we won't always be surrounded by wild cards who are "pulling their own weight." Keeping our balance, no matter what comes, is hard enough. **But it's harder if we lean over and attempt to help others too much, maybe bending, stooping, straining and maybe getting "pushed out of shape."** We can make it even harder for ourselves if we habitually blame those we're trying to help because **we ourselves** can't stand up straight.

It seems apparent to me that **the favor we do our fellow strugglers in the parade is to focus on our own balance**...and keep it as much as possible.

Chapter 26

Taking things personally

If we get off the parade, maybe pushed to the sidelines, we may start "running around in circles." We've trapped ourselves as we can't make things better when we're constantly "taking things personally" (judging and feeling hurt by our interpretations that others aren't helping **enough**).

Here are some examples of the circles which become traps.

We'll say you're hurt because a friend won't take your advice (so you can feel like a "good guy," wise and wonderful). So you sulk and "look daggers" at your friend. What does your friend do? Stay away, probably. So what do you do? Maybe you'll vow to show her she made a mistake to insult you the way she did. So when your friend later asks a favor, you refuse. It's easy to tell yourself this: "After the way she treated me, I'll make sure I never do anything for her."

Another example. We'll say you've used enough threats that you've forced those around you to help you. (Yes, you'd rather they'd have helped you willingly, but this is better than nothing.) **But because the others are off balance and leaning over to help you, before very long you'll probably regret being surrounded by bent-out-of-shape people.**

A mother believes that her kids never listen until she yells. And the more she yells, the more her kids "tune her out." Once she's given up looking for willingly-given co-operation, she's in no position to find out how to get it.

It's interesting that our speech style indicates to others that we're trapped because we're "taking things personally."

For example, when we're spinning inside this kind of trap, we often add the words "to me" to what we say. We wouldn't ask, "Why did they do this?" Instead we'd ask, "Why did they do this **to me**?" It's as if everything is judged and all decisions are made **with us in mind.** We can't see that others may do what they do to keep their own balance **for reasons which may have nothing to do with us.**

Maybe we'll ask, "Why do I deserve this?" It's as if we're the focus of everything that happens. We talk about "being taken advantage of...used...made to look like a fool."

We use this language when we can't see ourselves as making our own decisions. We're unable to say, simply, "I don't like the way that turned out...I'm not going to do that again."

We're trapped, as we're hurting most of the time, truly believing that we're being used and everybody's against us. So we believe we're helpless to make things better.

To get relief from the pain of our helplessness, a common way is to play even more helpless. We know from experience that at least a few others will usually reach out to help us (show their caring, "proof," at last, of our goodness).

Helplessness is an easy game to play, as it's not hard to learn "poor me" language. And as long as there's someone to be seduced into trying to help us, **all we have to do is continually make a stronger case.** But the trap gets tighter, as the more we play our helpless act, the more we actually become helpless.

And we can only tighten this trap so much, as each day is bringing more pain and despair. Even those trying to help us are getting increasingly uncomfortable with their failed attempts to prevent our downhill slide. And they're pulling away. We're alone again.

When our "taking things personally" keeps us locked in too many circular traps, and if we become convinced that things aren't ever going to get any better, this can lead to suicide…or murder.

Both can come from efforts to get relief from unendurable pain because we can't get the help and cooperation we keep expecting. And both can come from efforts to strike out at those we believe are causing the pain: "They'll be sorry for what they've done to me."

Chapter 27

Acceptance and appreciation

To escape circular traps, I think we can learn to see the world differently. We can look ahead, make our most accurate observations, **accept** what we see (that it's a shifting-sand world)...and process the information. Only after we've done that can we decide where to go so we can be effective.

I'm thinking especially about **acceptance**, as I believe that's what we particularly want of each other. After all, I'm the only me I can be at this minute, and you're the only you you can be.

But I'm thinking now about **self-acceptance,** and how hard it is to accept ourselves with our great limitations...and how much it helps when others are accepting of us.

However, we really want more than just acceptance. Whatever the label we use for what else we want, for now I'll call it appreciation. And we expect it from at least a few people. We may be aware that they can't help us **directly** in keeping our balance, but **we want them to at least care how our balancing efforts are going.**

I'm thinking again of our perennial struggles for self-acceptance. And this is what's interesting: We know how much others' acceptance means to us, **but we also know how stingy we tend to be in giving that same acceptance to others.**

Instead, our non-acceptance is often plain to see. We continually say to each other, "It would be so much better (for your own good, of course), if you'd do this instead of that...Why don't you do things more my way?...Why aren't you thinking more like me?"

It's as if our habitual implication is this: "My garbage heap is superior to yours. Why don't you just toss yours aside and use mine?"

If this non-acceptance is directed at other

people, situations and things, **we call it anger.** And the labels range from mild resentment to roaring rage.

But if the non-acceptance is directed at ourselves, **we call it guilt** (self-anger).

I used to think that people who were hurt and angry all the time were primarily angry **either** at themselves **or** others. But now I think that the anger is usually at both simultaneously.

Whether we call what we're living with self-anger, non-acceptance or guilt, our theories about the "cure" are usually the same: **We've got to work harder.**

Yet with this starting point, we just spin faster in the same circles. Because we're still failing to make things better, we get madder at **others** (and they stay further away). Or we get madder at **ourselves** because we must not deserve any better treatment…yet. (Then our self-anger/guilt/non-acceptance makes us even less effective. So we focus, **even more, on what's missing.**)

Pain seems to be everywhere, and especially it's the pain of not knowing what's wrong. ("Up to snuff?" What's that? Where is it? Does everyone know but me?) We keep torturing ourselves with the same questions: **"What's wrong with me? What am I doing wrong?"**

We're trapped, again and again, and to feel better about ourselves, maybe we'll try the "cure" of exaggerating our achievements (to ourselves as well as others). But others insist upon spoiling our illusions, and maybe they walk away muttering, "That old windbag."

Alone again. Hurting again. Obviously a stronger cure is needed. Stronger exaggerations? **Trying harder?**

Chapter 28

Not crazy?

I see us as going through our lives trying to figure out how to get the acceptance and appreciation we crave. We want so much to tell others (so they'll believe us) that we're really all right (and that we belong at least up to street level in the parade).

But how do we ourselves know that we're all right? **We can choose to believe that we are, and that's the method I'm suggesting.**

But we can't deny that comparing notes with others also feels good. We'll say that you ask me this: "Did you see what I saw over there?" And I'd answer,"Yes…I could hardly believe my eyes." And then you'd breathe a sigh of relief, "I thought I was really seeing things…guess I'm not so crazy after all."

Sometimes I think those few words say what we're trying to hear more often, that we're really not crazy.

But beyond that, maybe much of our conversation could be boiled down to just two words: "Appreciate me...appreciate me... appreciate me...(**then** I'll know **for sure** that I'm all right)."

We just can't give up trying to make a case for ourselves. Surely, someday we can make it, show 'em we've "got a leg to stand on"... occasionally...if the wind is blowing just right.

But we know it's easiest to try to get through to others when they truly care to hear us. Then we can relax and search through our garbage heap for the best words. And we'll persist even when we're stuttering and bumbling.

How many people will listen long enough that we can get out what we really want to say? Can anyone listen enough? And if they do, can we make any sense? (This is especially difficult when we're trying to explain why we did something last week ...and it didn't quite make sense even then.)

Chapter 29

We can't listen if...

How do we get others to listen to us?

We've got a better chance **if we listen to them first.** How do we get ourselves in shape so we're able to listen?

This entire book is my answer to that question.

We just can't listen if our futile struggles **for what we're missing** keep our garbage heap in turmoil.

We just can't listen if we're eternally defending ourselves in our fights against that shifting sand...and continually losing our balance.

We just can't listen if we're hurt and confused because we expect to be able to understand others and be understood by them.

We just can't listen if we're afraid of what we'll hear, "taking everything personally," and fighting the conclusion that we must be bad.

We just can't listen if we habitually feel guilty, that it's our fault the other person feels bad (**and we really ought to be different so the other will feel better**).

Maybe it doesn't matter exactly which route we've taken to non-listening. But once we've reached that place, just about every kind of problem is intensified.

Here are just a few of the consequences of non-listening (or maybe what's called **selective listening**).

Because others feel helpless in getting through to us, they eventually quit trying. **And they also become unwilling to listen to us.**

Another result of non-listening is that we're forced to live mostly with our guesses.

By making decisions based on unflattering theories about those we believe are hurting us, we guarantee that our problem solving will be failing: "Anybody who'd do that to me must hate me...I'll fix 'em... "

But because we're hurting **more**, we're trying **more**, and our non-listening guesses lead to **more** hurt and **more** disappointment... and **more** rounds of **more** power struggles: **"I can't live with myself if I let 'em treat me like that..."**

Chapter 30

Hearing feelings

Even if we realize the importance of really listening, and we're able to feel good enough about ourselves that we can actually do it, there's still one more thing. And that's remembering that speakers want to hear a response that shows they've actually been heard. And what's wanted may be a response that shows **feelings** are being heard.

Often I hear these words: "My partner says I don't listen...but I do...and I can repeat back exactly what he says... "

It's apparent to me that the partner is missing evidence of getting **feelings** heard.

But when we're speaking, we don't always make it easy for others to hear our feelings. And sometimes we deliberately hide them.

For example, maybe others are telling us about something they've done, and somewhere in the middle they'll tuck in a tiny remark about a feeling. (Maybe even with a smile to cover it if it's especially painful.)

As listeners, if we don't pick up that tiny feeling and comment on it **before** making other responses, all discussion may stop. Especially if the speakers are those who habitually are "taking things personally," they may block out hearing anything after the point at which they felt slighted: "They never did care about my feelings...They never listen... What's the use of trying to tell them anything?"

Because it's so important for our own well-being to be able and willing to hear others, and especially their feelings, I'm going to emphasize this point.

I'd been listening to a woman in the counseling room when I became seriously alarmed for her safety. **She obviously believed she didn't need to listen, and it was clear that those around her weren't getting through to her.** [I'll pause for a moment for a side comment. Many times people "act as if they know it all," and I usually see this as overcompensation for their fears of the opposite. But in the case of the woman I'm writing about, it seemed that she truly believed that she had all the information she'd ever need, and she was totally capable of pronouncing judgments on everything and everybody.]

After the woman had talked for only a half hour, I did something unusual. I stopped her, and I said this: "I'm guessing that you're in real danger. The people around you can't be feeling good about you when they can't get through to you."

This is her exact response: "That's true. In my husband's prayer this morning at breakfast, he asked God's permission to kill me."

getting through **without** anger

acceptance
appreciation

not getting
through

anger

getting through
with anger

isolation

Chapter 31

Getting through to each other

These sketches show my attempt to lay out an overview of our efforts to get through to each other.

The first circle shows that getting through (at least somewhat), can lead to getting acceptance and appreciation...and back around to getting through...

I'm trying to get through to you now. Because what I'm saying is so foreign to so many people, I know I need the best writing skills I can muster. That's because my primary goal is to compare notes with you and see if you're seeing what I'm seeing.

This means I need to write slowly and as accurately as possible. You know from your reading so far, that I think getting through, even a little, is rare.

Recently I was standing in a cafeteria line when someone mentioned one of my earlier books, SHAKE THE ANGER HABIT! (written with Pat Rooney). The person next to me immediately responded: "That title doesn't make any sense to me...Most people I know are just learning to get their anger out...The last thing they need is to bury their anger...or believe it's bad."

What was I to say? In that setting, I don't think I could have said anything to prove that I wasn't crazy. So I didn't try.

In the back of this book I've listed some suggestions for getting through to each other without getting angry. But my main point here is that **maybe** getting through is impossible **most** of the time. In the counseling room, it's clear that few people realize how hard it is. For example, I sometimes hear this: "I never repeat myself...if they don't get it the first time, they don't get another chance."

getting through **without** anger

acceptance appreciation

not getting through

anger

getting through **with** anger

isolation

For myself, I've found that getting through (just getting a fair hearing) means that I have to try in **many** ways and at **many** times. It's clear that the burden of learning to get through (as much as possible) **is on me.** Writing books and publishing them isn't easy, but it works. It feels awfully good to get through **some** times and in **some** places... and get **some** feedback.

The second circle shows what happens when we're habitually off balance. And instead of accepting the burden of figuring out how we can get through, **we get mad at those who won't listen to us.** And of course that doesn't help. They stay away and listen even less. So we justify getting madder, around and around the circle.

For example, a person might complain: "I've asked 'em time and time again not to do that...they don't listen...they don't see how important this is to me..."

This speaker's definition of getting through would be this: "Getting through means **getting what I expect.**" In a world of shifting sand, it's obvious this person is spending a lot of time being angry...pushing others away...and justifying anger because others have pulled away (maybe so far away that it's impossible to get through to them at all).

The third circle shows that we can always get through **if we get angry enough.** By "throwing our weight around," we can have impact, at last: "They've got to reckon with me...they can't ignore me and get away with it...they'd better do what I say or else..."

But every time we use anger to get through, it's as if we're using **a knife to the heart.** Yes, we do get through, but we're paying an awfully high price: **isolation.**

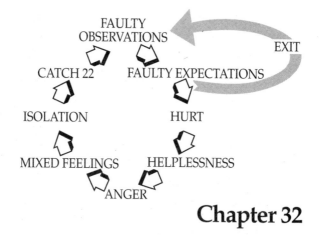

Chapter 32

The anger trap

Let's look at the way an anger trap keeps us trapped.

❏❏❏Faulty Observations: We enter the trap if we aren't seeing how fragile the wild cards are. So we keep telling ourselves that we ought to be getting more help (co-operation, acceptance, appreciation).

❏❏❏Faulty Expectations: Based on our faulty observations, we keep expecting the help that's missing…and being disappointed.

The Exit: Here's the way out of the trap. Every time (and I mean **every**

time) we don't get what we expect, we can get out of the trap by asking ourselves this question: **What's wrong with my observations that I keep expecting one thing and getting another?** Once we've switched to **focusing on and correcting our own observations,** everything is different. Now that our eyes are open, we're defining problems better, moving in the parade and continuing to check and re-check our observations. Because we're outside the trap, with heads up, we stay in a starting position for more and more effective problem solving.

❏❏❏**Hurt:** If we stay inside the trap, absolutely certain that our judgment is accurate that we ought to get more help (cooperation, acceptance, appreciation), we keep our eyes half closed, with heads down, and continue to tell ourselves how justified we are to feel hurt.

A man at a workshop here was asking me how to avoid feeling hurt: "It's just as

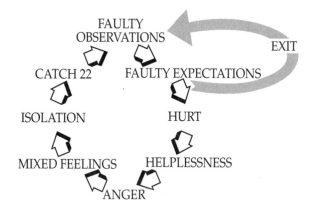

FAULTY
OBSERVATIONS

CATCH 22   FAULTY EXPECTATIONS

ISOLATION   HURT

MIXED FEELINGS   HELPLESSNESS

ANGER

EXIT

if it grabs me suddenly…like it comes out of the air."

I agreed that it seems that way, but I also told him that I see hurt as coming from what we expect. He said that he realized that his hurting was irrational, and this is the example he gave:

"I feel hurt every afternoon because my wife won't have the door unlocked when I get home from work. I know she cares for me and she doesn't want me to be hurt. Why can't she be standing there with the door unlocked when I get home?"

It's as if the man is saying this: "I choose to hurt unless my wife will do what I've begged her to do. It isn't too much to expect her to set a timer every day so she can be in the entrance hall when I get home. Then all she'd have to do would be to flip that door unlocked when she hears me coming up the steps."

What's interesting is that the man could choose to be hurt if his wife didn't do fifty other things when he got home (just so he could get "proof" she cares for him). **But what the man wasn't seeing is that his wife has to keep her balance in her own way. If he chooses to be hurt because of his faulty observations of the way she ought to be, he'll continue to hurt.**

❏❏❏ **Helplessness:** At this point, when we're spinning around inside the trap, we realize that nothing is working to get the help (cooperation, acceptance, appreciation) we keep expecting. We are truly helpless. We've already tried niceness and meanness, and neither is strong enough to get others to lose their balance for long. But helplessness is extremely painful. And too often we'd rather do the wrong thing in an attempt to get power rather than do nothing.

❏❏❏ **Anger:** Anger is one of the wrong things, as we hurt ourselves in the long run.

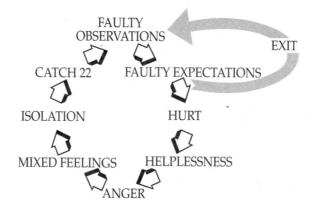

FAULTY
OBSERVATIONS

EXIT

CATCH 22   FAULTY EXPECTATIONS

ISOLATION   HURT

MIXED FEELINGS   HELPLESSNESS

ANGER

Even if we're only plotting revenge silently, we can believe we're more powerful than if we're doing nothing.

But when we don't want to be silent, and we decide to let others know we're angry with them (for not helping), we're in one more power struggle.

Then the louder the voice we use, the better, probably with actions to match.

Can we get real power from such efforts? If you look at the top of the trap (at the faulty observations), you'll remember that what we're trying to get is more help (cooperation, acceptance, appreciation). **But we want it willingly given. And there's no way we can get it willingly given by way of anger.**

To make things worse, no matter how much we use anger to get what we want, **we can never know, for sure, if others are giving it to us because they really care for us…or because they're afraid of our anger. So nothing we get feels good.**

⬜⬜⬜ **Mixed feelings:** We've thrown our big fit, and we had to do it, didn't we? We couldn't let 'em get away with that, could we? But why don't we feel better afterwards? Why do we feel worse? It hurts so much to see others cringe when we approach. All we seem to have done is get even more proof of our "badness."

⬜⬜⬜ **Isolation:** As far as I can tell, going around in the trap guarantees that we'll eventually become isolated. It doesn't make any difference how the isolation occurs, whether we leave others or they leave us, or whether the isolation is physical or mental. But eventually we'll be standing alone…rejected…feeling like an outcast.

If we look at the top of the circle, we can see that we got ourselves into the trap because of our faulty observations (that we ought to be getting more help, cooperation, acceptance, and appreciation).

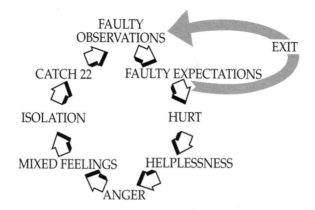

Once we habitually believe that, and habitually spin around in the trap to the point of isolation, each time feels worse.

When the pain becomes intolerable, this is where alcohol, drugs and maybe suicide come in. Or maybe we'll choose to live in a fantasy world. There's no shortage of suggested "cures," and it's fortunate that there's no shortage. That's because we'll keep needing new ones as the old ones continue to fail.

One of the most common "cures" comes from the belief that we can turn off our feelings and avoid pain. So we go numb, as if we're pulling a plug so the feelings can't flow through to hurt us.

But the problem is that by cutting off receiving any bad feelings, we've also cut off receiving any good feelings.

Often a person in the counseling room will say this: "All I want is to be happy." Advice-givers often tell such a person they need to do more for themselves (and not so much for the "bad guys" in their lives who obviously aren't reciprocating). Yet the person usually gives this sad response: "But I don't know what I want to do."

When a person becomes numb enough, that's the only answer they're able to give.

We pay an awfully high price for this numbness. For one thing, we don't realize that those around us are probably operating at a feeling level. When they talk, it's hard for us to show them they're getting through to us. We haven't really heard their feelings, and when we respond, it's by talking facts.

Others are not only uncomfortable when we can't hear their feelings, but we put ourselves in danger of their attempts to get through to us. The knives to the heart. Or just needles.

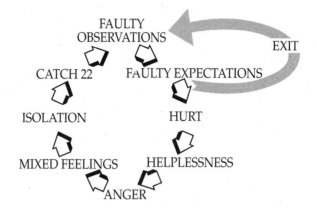

FAULTY
OBSERVATIONS

EXIT

CATCH 22   FAULTY EXPECTATIONS

ISOLATION   HURT

MIXED FEELINGS   HELPLESSNESS

ANGER

When we turn off our feelings even more to avoid feeling the danger, the danger increases as our numbness increases. And when others ask how we feel (maybe demand to know), we can't respond, as we truly don't know.

But there's another price we pay for our tuning out. We miss the guidance for running our lives that we'd be getting from recognizing our feelings. Maybe the words we use to talk about feelings are just attempts to summarize what's happening to us internally and externally. But if we don't recognize the feelings, we miss the messages. For example, "Beware: run for your life!" What if we've pulled the plug and don't get the message?

In isolation we're trying to avoid others' disapproval, as we can't tolerate feeling even more of a "bad guy" than we already do. But this means we have to please everybody (an impossible job) in order to believe we deserve help and cooperation. **So we have trouble telling the truth, even to ourselves. But this leads to more pain and confusion.**

At some point, we realize that nowhere is safe. We've become so afraid of even the tiniest criticism that we can hardly function.

In our terror of too much isolation, we may feel forced to come out of our near-paralysis and go back to trying niceness or meanness again. Yet we know in advance that our efforts will fail. But we also know that the **attacks and counter-attacks of power struggles prove that we're not alone...and whatever the resulting turmoil, it's better than too much isolation.**

Before leaving this spot in the trap, I want to comment on the common belief that it's helpful to get our anger out.

Maybe you've noticed that I've bypassed

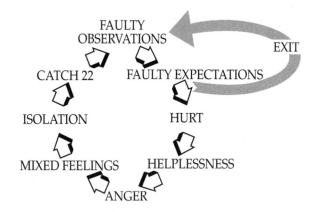

the need to make decisions about whether it's best to bury anger...or get it out. In this book I'm addressing the **kind of thinking** we use to justify getting angry. What I'm suggesting is that we can form another habit instead, that of seeing each other as struggling to keep balanced. And then it becomes clear that we don't deserve each others' anger.

I think we hurt ourselves, repeatedly, when we truly believe our anger is justified. **But I think we hurt ourselves even more by accepting the theory that we ought to get our anger out.**

Here's an example of what I believe is carrying this theory too far. I keep hearing of women's groups that meet solely for the purpose of shouting obscenities in unison at males they perceive to be oppressing them. (Maybe men's groups are doing something similar, and I just haven't heard of it.)

I don't see anything more in this than a releasing of physical tension...temporarily. And I don't think it gives any real relief if we're continuing to **justify** our anger...and forming it again and again.

I may be the only person anywhere who is skeptical of the theory that getting anger out is good.

Actually, the **only** way I see that getting anger out works for us...in the long run...is **if our goal is to be isolated.**

One of the most harmful prevailing myths about anger, from my point of view, is that we ought to get our anger out **as a cure for depression (numbness).**

Friends are telling each other this: "You've got to stand up on your own two feet and tell 'em off...put your foot down."

All I see in this kind of advice is the possibility of changing sides in a power struggle. So the "upper hand" is reversed?

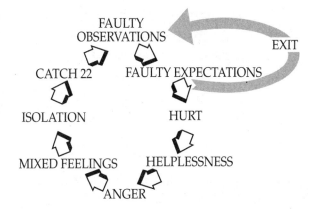

FAULTY OBSERVATIONS

CATCH 22

FAULTY EXPECTATIONS

EXIT

ISOLATION

HURT

MIXED FEELINGS

HELPLESSNESS

ANGER

Can the "winner" really enjoy the change... and the constant fear of being toppled at the most unexpected moment?

Advice-givers telling others to get their anger out evidently don't realize that those not doing so have a good reason: they've found it doesn't work... **for them** in the long run. (The bigger the build-up, the bigger the explosion, and the bigger the danger.)

But back to anger as a "cure" for depression. It's easy to see how bystanders may believe that when a person is numb (depressed), that a person's getting angry might bring them back to life. So the belief flourishes that anger and depression are opposites.

But it's my observation that anger and depression go together. Sometimes I see people who are so numb that they tell me their anger is the only feeling they can feel. And to combat total numbness, they actually fan the flames of their anger… as that's better than feeling nothing.

From what I can tell, nothing, **including numbness,** gets better when we get our anger out… except for **temporary** relief of physical tension. But attending to the brush fires sparked by our anger may not be worth the price. Because brushfires spread while our back is turned, the vigilance necessary to protect ourselves creates more tension.

Then we seek **more** relief from **more** tension by getting **more** anger out **more** often.

Often I'm asked if anger is a good motivator for getting us to do something we wouldn't have done otherwise. Here's my answer: I think it's extremely unlikely that what we'd do out of anger would really help us in the long run.

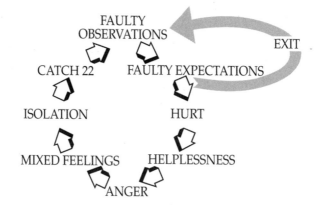

FAULTY OBSERVATIONS

FAULTY EXPECTATIONS

CATCH 22

EXIT

ISOLATION

HURT

MIXED FEELINGS

HELPLESSNESS

ANGER

☐☐☐ **Catch 22:** I call this a Catch 22 to show how the trap is a trap. We just can't make better observations in order to get out of the trap from a position of isolation. Yet without better observations, we can't escape the trap: so we stay isolated. Who will tell us the truth if it makes us angry? Who will stay close if we're alternating between niceness and anger? How can we ever do enough to avoid others' anger? What's wrong? What's wrong?

You can see how easy it is to get stuck whirling around inside the trap, each time arriving at the same point: **isolation.**

By looking at the trap the way I'm suggesting, we can see that **there really is an exit.**

Chapter 33

Closing the first counseling session

If you'd actually been listening to all this in the counseling room, you'd probably need a break by this time. First sessions usually end soon after I've presented the anger trap.

In **Part II** of this book, you'll read more about the questions I usually get in a follow-up session.

In the initial session, I've purposely been turning aside questions, especially the ones that start this way: "What should I do when…" That's because I was busy laying the groundwork to show that we can't find satisfactory answers to such questions unless we break the power-struggle mindset. Even though I've personalized my presentation for each person (instead of giving it the way it reads here), there probably have been gaps. To cover them, I hand out copies of SHAKE THE ANGER HABIT! and maybe a pamphlet for couples. (The pamphlet is included in this book, Supplement #3.)

Sometimes, before ending the session, I'll do some guided imagery, just for relaxation.

I'm aware that it's not easy to absorb and sort out all I've presented. And for some, it may be truly overwhelming.

Follow-up appointments are usually set a week after the first. **Before you read Part II, you too may want to wait a week.**

PART II

Chapter 34

Follow-up session, comments and questions

In the second part of this book, I'll tell you a little about the follow-up sessions here. Again I listen to each person, with my head down, for approximately two hours.

Just one man's feedback: "I came in here as low as it's possible to get, an outcast...and I shot up like a rocket."

More often I hear this, expressed in innumerable ways: "Everything's better."

What's interesting to me is that it's rare to hear a person who can explain how they're getting such different results.

All I can really tell is that each person's thinking has been changing. And the "I've-tried-everything" talk has completely disappeared.

Evidently the different thinking is all that's needed as a first step toward **going in a different direction.** And then the rewards become exciting. I suspect that each person is simply learning to be at least a **little** more accepting of themselves and others. Then whatever they're doing is a **little** less stressful, and others are a **little** more comfortable with them.

It doesn't take much of a change in direction to be exciting after facing a dead-end.

Will there be wrong turns? Of course. But the difference is that each person has learned, **from their own experience,** that they're able to get up after a fall and "get back on track."

Many times, in a first session, someone will have been repeatedly saying this: "I know I can't change others, as the only person I can change is myself."

But by the second session, they can see that they'd been using that saying to justify self-anger. And that had led them to "bad guy" feelings, which led to more attempts to prove what they didn't have to prove… which led to more "bad guy" feelings…

A man last night told me he'd made a big decision. He'd thrown away his knife, his baseball bat and his black felt hat (the one he'd worn pulled down, nearly over his eyes, the entire first counseling session).

At the first session he'd spent most of his time berating himself for being some kind of an ogre. He must have been tremendously shocked to get a glimmer of this truth: **It was only his own belief that he was bad…and what he thought he had to do to prove the opposite…which was creating his problems.**

Chapter 35

What if we can't choose to believe?

Some people ask what to do if they can't believe they're doing their best all the time.

When I hear this question, I remind myself that we all choose what we believe... **for our own reasons.** All I can do from the sidelines is show that we get different results according to what we choose to believe. (And I have to keep repeating that I'm not talking about facts.)

If you're one who has trouble accepting that you're doing the best you can all the time, tell yourself that it's all right to be where you are...right now. Since you need a starting place, this is it. It's obviously right for you...right now. That's self-acceptance.

And once you've found that starting place, you can move in the direction you choose.

You may find, for example, that you can easily switch back and forth from accepting yourself as doing your best...to the opposite. And in each case, you'll find that you can accept wherever you are as right for you... at that minute. You're the only one making the choices, and you're the only one who can decide which results you like best.

You might ask, **"But what if I'm fooling myself, just telling myself that I'm doing my best when it isn't true?"** You can choose to believe that if you want to, and also accept that your choice is right for you. But I think it helps to remind yourself, again and again, that you're not talking about facts.

Maybe you're one who says you'd be selfish if you focused so much on keeping your own balance. You can choose to believe that if you want to. For myself, I believe that when I keep balanced, and don't need to lean on others, I'm in the best possible position to be truly cooperative and considerate...the exact opposite of selfish.

Pat Rooney, co-author of SHAKE THE ANGER HABIT! and THE ANGER PUZZLE, had difficulty accepting that we're all doing the best we can. When we'd do workshops together, he'd emphasize a point which I consistently missed.

He said he finally realized that his earlier trouble in believing that we're all doing our best was his belief that his ex-wife wasn't. The way he saw it, she obviously wasn't doing the best she could **for him.** It had taken awhile for Pat to realize that she had to do her best for **herself** and for **her** own balance.

Pat's problem had come from the fact that he'd been trying to please others for so long that he assumed others were doing the same. And his ex-wife just wasn't trying hard enough...**to please him.**

Chapter 36

Others' anger

Many people ask about handling other people's anger.

Actually, I think the most important thing I've learned, from seeing anger as I do, is that it makes it really easy to see that an angry person is going around inside **their own** trap.

Seeing this helps me to be able to breathe deeply and keep my own balance. Then I can actually listen to the angry person, whether the anger is directed at me or someone else.

Usually I can hear the angry person's pain, pain that the world just won't be different (more nourishing, more support-ive, and the way it seems it really ought to be).

You'll probably remember that when I call anger a "knife to the heart," I'm suggesting it's a tool we use to get through to another when we're desperate. So I think it's **extremely important** that we **really listen** to an angry person.

But what can we do after we've listened and felt the blast of another's anger? To find the answer to that question, I think it helps to be aware of how we ourselves feel after we've "let off steam."

Mostly, I think we want to be left alone to sort out our own feelings. And that means being safe from another's crowding, prodding, or condemning. But there's a conflict here. **At the same time,** we may want someone available so we can get assurance that we haven't isolated ourselves...totally.

It's easy to know what not to do in response to another's anger. For example, I think you see the danger in what a woman said last week: "When my husband yells, I just laugh."

Also, it doesn't help, at all, for the one who's the target of anger to be defensive and respond with facts and details.

For example, a man is jealous, and after his partner's been away from home, he may habitually say this: "I can't stand it...I'm afraid I'm not good enough for you...You'd go off with anyone who asks you...You're just looking for a chance to get away...You hurt me every time you can...You're bad, wrong, just like your mother/sister/friend..."

It's easy to see that the man is making it harder to get reassurance that he won't be totally isolated. And it's no help if his partner is responding with facts. "I just went to the store because we were out of... "

Because the man is talking about **himself,** and his own fears, his partner's stating facts won't be comforting. He's probably thinking something like this: **"She doesn't really care about my feelings...**I've got to watch her closer...She's still trying to get away."

After each harangue, as the woman becomes more distraught and less inclined to give the assurance her husband is seeking, he pushes harder. And by that time he may accurately be sensing that his wife truly is moving away from him...even if only mentally.

What happens if the wife feels good enough about herself that she can breathe deeply and know she's doing her best, and **then just listens?** Everything is different, as then she can visualize her husband going around inside the anger trap...again. And she can remember that he really is doing the best he can, at that minute. When she responds, (maybe much later), **just because** she's truly heard his feelings, any exchange which follows at least has a **chance** of being productive .

What I've been describing is an extremely common power struggle with couples. I hope you can see that it's what **both** are doing which perpetuates the pattern. And just one person's changing can break that pattern.

Maybe a wife will ask me this: "Don't I have a right to defend myself?"

Yes, she can defend herself, and she may use many different ways. But to be effective, she won't be trying to get through to her husband while he's so consumed with his own terrors that he can't listen.

So what can she do that's effective?

Step one, as I see it, is focusing on keeping her own balance. And that means avoiding being defensive (off balance) by remembering that no one else can **ever** know what decisions are best **for her**...at any one minute. Remembering that means that she doesn't have to apologize or pass out with shame, or fight back, just because another person thinks the opposite and insists on telling her about it.

For step two, whatever she does, she'll be **more likely** to be effective...**just because she's starting from a balanced position.**

Chapter 37

A couple's experience

A woman in the counseling room was crying as she was talking about her husband: "How can he say he loves me when he says that talking to me is like talking to a blank wall?"

She'd been telling me that her husband was spending so much time in bars that he was rarely home. And when he did stay home, she was afraid that she'd say the wrong thing and he'd leave. So she was tiptoeing around and saying practically nothing.

Later, when her husband was in the counseling room, he offered this information in his opening statement. "All my life I've been this way. The one thing I can't stand is to see a woman cry." The man went on to explain that even though he wasn't much of a drinker, he'd rather spend his evenings in bars talking to strangers than to be at home where his wife would cry because he wanted her to talk to him.

After he and his wife had their individual appointments, the man told me this: **"We've talked more in the last week than in all the ten years we've been married."**

What made the difference? It's not hard to see that such a change could happen instantly when each felt good enough about **themselves** that they could listen. They no longer had to "take things personally" and live only with their own interpretations of what was happening.

Let's look closer.

The husband obviously interpreted his wife's fear of talking to him as rejection, and his conclusion was that he must be some kind of a "bad guy." Seeing her cry was simply too much "proof" of his "badness." **So he felt forced to withdraw.**

Obviously the woman saw "proof" of her "badness" in that her husband didn't want to be with her. Since she couldn't risk seeing more "proof," **she felt forced to withdraw.**

In the pattern the two were in, it had been impossible for either to see that the behavior of the other **wasn't** for lack of caring, but the opposite. Just by seeing each other as trying to keep balanced, they could see that it was **their own** interpretation of **their own** "proof" of **their own** "badness" which had caused the problem.

Chapter 38

Quiz for readers

All you'll need for this quiz is a paper and pencil and your best imagination.

We'll say you have a habit of taking things personally. And you're feeling hurt over someone's behavior toward you.

Step 1: Make a list of explanations for the other's behavior, the longer the better: "She must have been mad about what I said about her boyfriend...She always hated me and I've just been too dumb to know it...She doesn't even know what she's doing half the time."

Step 2: Decide which **one** explanation you think is best, then decide what action you'd take if that **one** explanation were accurate.

Step 3: Look at the other explanations on your list, then plan your action for each one, just as if it might be accurate.

Step 4: In Chapter 11 there's a story about a man who had just bought a new car. Later, when rocks were being thrown on top of his car, he found he was mistaken in believing that the rock-thrower was out to hurt him.

> **Question:** When the man learned that he was mistaken about what he thought was happening, where did his anger go? If it disappeared, **how fast did it happen?**

Step 5: In Chapter 12 there's a story about a depressed woman who would get mad when her friend wouldn't come over and sit with her. She concluded that her friend didn't care for her, and only later learned that the friend hadn't come to her place because she couldn't climb the stairs.

> **Question:** When the woman found she had misinterpreted

her friend's behavior, where did her anger go? If it disappeared, **how fast did it happen?**

Step 6: Ask yourself this question: If you continually make your very best observations, **do you think you'll find that all hurt and anger are formed because we don't (and can't) understand what's really going on?**

Chapter 39

One man's experience

Many people summarize their feelings by saying that they feel lost.

A man told me that last night, and I'll give you a bare outline of his situation.

The man is exceptionally verbal and easily "covered all the bases" of what I've been writing about. The session ran a full four hours, and as I'm writing this, I'm looking forward to his feedback at his follow-up session.

He's in his late twenties and is unusually nice looking. He's terribly afraid of disapproval, and he couldn't come in without attributing his visit to a son's trouble in school.

He's read a tremendous number of self-help books, is in AA (and his wife is in Al Anon).

He's presently quite numb and trying to stay that way to escape his misery. Because he's numb, his wife complains about his insensitivity.

He can't risk telling the truth as someone might **possibly** get mad at him. He consistently feels so low that it's as if he lives in fear of one more "hit" which would be **totally** devastating.

He's presently working for his dad, and it bothers him that his dad is a practicing alcoholic. But he's afraid he can't make it elsewhere. He's searched for many years, and in many ways and places, for a belief system which would bring relief from his misery.

Until he overdid it, he was exercising to get relief from nearly intolerable tension. He rarely smiles, and he resists looking into a mirror as he thinks the person he'd see wouldn't be real. He feels detached from everyone except his one-year old daughter.

He's believed that he's a bad guy since he was about ten years old. That was when he became aware of a dark presence which seemed to get inside him and never leave (a monster? a pool of poison?). Because he can't get understanding (his label for what's missing), he always feels that he's an outsider. So he's spent his life trying harder and harder to conform in order to get the acceptance and understanding **he believes will make him happy.**

He's in a quiet rage at his helplessness to make things better. And he spends a great deal of time in fantasies of power: "I'll force you to respect me ..."

In spite of his attempts to stay numb, his hurt is so intense that he can hardly function. He's almost totally convinced that no matter how hard he tries, he'll never feel better.

It's sad for me to realize that as long as he stays focused on what's missing **(the help and understanding he's been seeking for so long),** the more his failures are inevitable.

Many people would zero in on the man's rage and encourage him to get it out. It's my observation that this isn't necessary at all. What I see is that when people are seeing the world **today** so they aren't angry **today,** the old anger slips into the background. And from all I can tell, it disappears. What I see is that it takes **thinking** to justify anger, even **old** anger, and that **thinking can change instantly.**

What I expect to hear from the man in a follow-up session is that he's confirmed, **by his own experience,** how he has been hurting himself: He was focusing on what was ·missing, constantly fighting for the help and understanding he kept expecting. That's what had been keeping him unable to focus on what he's got, every minute. And being **unable to find that starting place,** he couldn't move effectively. So he'd pulled tighter and tighter into himself rather than risk more failures.

Two weeks later

I've just finished the follow-up session, and I'm feeling overwhelmed with trying to summarize another four hours. So I'll talk about myself instead. For one thing, it's always exciting to see someone go from being off balance to something completely different. And since this man talked quite a bit about SHAKE THE ANGER HABIT!, I'm reminding myself how valuable it is to have reading material to reinforce the first session.

⁘

The first thing the man said was that things were completely different with his boy. (Even though it was a school problem with the boy which had prompted the man's first phone call here, he hadn't talked about that at all.) He also told me that he'd cut down on caffeine and sugar. After the first week of withdrawal, he said he's feeling more calm and is very happy about that.

He certainly sounded much more comfortable. It's my guess, that once his tension eased, he was able to **listen a little more,** and it wasn't so uphill to get through to those around him (so he could get a least a **little more** understanding).

Three days later

I'm still thinking about this man, and how I feel my reporting on these pages can say so little. I'm just **so** conscious of how hard it is to say what we really want to say. At this point I'll fall back on my own working theories, even though I well know the tendency for us to find what we're looking for. But here's what I see.

The man was truly desperate for power. **And power, to me, is being able to feel we're able to get through to each other, at least a little, when it's really important.**

The more the man became engrossed with himself and his search for the power to make things better, the more he was failing. When he was so absorbed in seeking relief from the pain of his failures, he couldn't do the one thing necessary to get real power: **listen to others first**…so he could get through to them.

A later note

Because the man needed forms for his insurance company, he stopped by and we talked another three hours. Essentially, he says that he'd heard all this before, but this is the first time he could apply it. (He did the fine-tuning.) The first thing he said was this: "It's like my eyes are bugged out trying to see everything." As you can guess, we had time to talk about the process here, his boy and his wife, and everything that he's seeing differently. Obviously he's making better observations and better decisions...**now that he's holding his head up.**

Chapter 40

A common power struggle with couples

This is the picture I get of most couples who come in.

Two people are hanging by their fingernails on the edge of a cliff. And both are blaming the other for not lending a hand.

Seeing this picture makes it clear that any method the two people use to get the other to "lend a hand" won't work. And if they believe they absolutely have to have the other's help, they'll stay stuck...or fall off the cliff.

I'll describe the most common form of a couple's power struggle that I see. (I'll call them husband and wife as that makes it easier to identify which is which. Throughout this book, however, I assume you've noticed that I'm not suggesting that sex differences play a part in anything I've been writing about.)

Both the husband and wife want the other to be different (more helpful). And this guarantees that both will feel somewhat inadequate and hurt that they aren't quite pleasing their partner. And they both blame the other for their unhappiness.

Because of the discomfort, they continually crave reassurance of the other's caring. And both have different methods of trying to get it.

We'll say the husband's way is to explode: "I can't stand it any more...you've got to do this...and you've got to stop doing that ... "

When his wife agrees to change for him, he'll interpret that as "proof" that she really cares for him.

Because the wife probably is risking her own balance to do what her husband wants, she'll probably go back to her old ways before long.

So battles are fought again and again … with the same result. The husband has "proof," for that brief time, that his wife really cares.

If that's the only way the husband knows how to get the changes ("proof" of caring) he seeks, the power struggles are certain to continue.

We'll say the wife uses different methods for trying to get her husband to change (so she can get "proof" of his caring). Maybe she'll use the "iron fist in the velvet glove" approach, maybe trying to be nicer and do more and more for her husband.

But she too explodes in anger whenever she finds (again as her husband does), that it isn't possible to be nice **enough** or do **enough** to get the desired "proof" (the other's changing and **staying changed**). But the wife's explosions cause her extreme anxiety. After all, isn't she supposed to be the nice one?

It's true that her explosion probably gets temporary changes (the "proof" of caring she's seeking from her husband), but **both** the husband and wife are increasingly uncomfortable with **both** their own and the other's explosions. Because **both** want even more reassurance to ease their growing discomfort, **both** fight even more to get it from the other. That's because it's obvious to **both** that they just haven't tried hard enough...**yet**...to get what's missing (however they label the "proof" they think they ought to be able to get).

By the time couples come here, the intervals between such power struggles have been getting shorter, and they describe this as being on a roller coaster. Even at the highest point, there's no real ecstasy, as they always know what's ahead.

(I wonder if this isn't more like being on a ferris wheel. But that image breaks down as I realize that for two people, probably involved in so many different power struggles with each other, they're always either up, down or in-between **all at the same time.**)

Probably for most couples, as the power struggles to get the other to change become more predictable, they're less scary. And maybe they lose momentum over the years.

Or maybe couples settle down to a pattern of mid-level anguish. They hang suspended between not being **too** miserable with each other, yet not able to be really happy...for fear of the next explosion.

Couples who stay together usually evolve into a problem-solving style in which one is more often the **pusher** and the other a **withdrawer.**

Recently, it seems I've had a "run" on seeing people who have withdrawn, too far, as a way of escaping a partner's pushing. This may be to the point of near suicide, or just into too much fantasy. One woman was in a wheelchair because she ached all over and couldn't walk, although extensive medical tests show nothing is physically wrong. (Again, I think of the image of walking in a parade, of falling down, and being afraid to get up.)

It must be extremely hard, from a down position, to see that partners are trying to make things better in the only way they know. Nothing hurts partners more than to

be accused by the other of "not even trying."
Translation: "You're not trying in the way **I think** you ought to be trying."

But once it's a habit to see the partner as a villain (obviously the bad one, the one who isn't even trying), the "solution" to the problem is easy: Search for a different partner (if only mentally), one who won't need to be pushed so much to give evidence of caring...one who will be willing to change ...**and stay changed**...without so much pushing. (By this time, mostly what **both** partners are seeing is the other's attacking and defending behavior. And neither looks good.)

From what I see, to escape the power-struggle trap, we can accept each other as equals. And this can happen only when we're comfortable enough **with ourselves** that we don't have to see another person as down so we can feel up. (The image of the parade, again, and being so afraid we're six inches under that we need to show everybody that we're really up above.)

I see people who are in such fear of their "badness" that they're desperate to show they're really good, so good they deserve special treatment. And in the counseling room, this may take the form of trying to prove that their problems are worse than all others. And maybe natural laws really ought to be suspended for them.

It isn't easy to learn to be accepting of a partner. When I look at my husband, I remind myself that I have to accept the whole package, as that's the only one he comes in. If I don't, I'm unable to relate to the only person he is…at this minute.

If I hadn't gone back to school and earned a license to listen to so many couples, I don't think our marriage would have survived. I feel tremendous compassion for those who desperately want to make their relationships better, but like me, just didn't know how to do it.

What I've learned is that it was my own learning to be more accepting which made the difference. Hard as it is to believe, repeatedly I see that it's just one person's learning to be more accepting which is the key to reducing tension. Because there's less defensiveness and the need to create crises to gain temporary "proof" of caring, we can stay off the old roller coaster.

Sometimes I'm asked this question: "But how do I get the other person to change if they're hurting me?"

Answer: Once I see that I don't have the power to change another person directly, all I can do is try to get cooperation. And how do I do that? **When I see that we're really equals, I'm projecting something completely different than if I see my partner as bad or wrong. Because my actions will be different, the reactions are different. I still can't predict what's ahead (in a shifting-sand world), but the old pattern is broken.**

Chapter 41

Implications for society

In this final chapter, I'm thinking of anger and power struggles, and of the tremendous amount of information I'm gathering every day. And I'm wondering how such information can be applied to society as a whole.

On talkshows, for years, I could count on getting this question: "As a society are we angrier than ever?" I didn't realize until recently that I'm no longer getting that question.

If you're like me, you're stunned at the rate of speed with which we're approaching a firestorm of rage and violence.

For a long time, as I've been appearing on talkshows, I've been saying this: "From what I know about anger and from the factors I see already in place, it looks as if our overall anger level will continue to rise."

I'll tell you where I see hope, and maybe you'll see what I see, that **all of us have the power to ease tension,** even if only a little at first. And who knows where we can go from such humble beginnings.

But first I'll make a few comments on the factors I see which are "fanning the flames" of anger. And I'll pose some questions.

We know that large numbers of people are angry, and that indicates to me they're probably feeling that they aren't getting through. (It's true, however, that their definition of getting through may include the impossible qualification that they get what they expect.) But for now, when I say that large numbers of people aren't getting through, I'm using the most ordinary definition of getting through, **being able to**

feel powerful, able to get comfort from knowing that others actually care to hear us …at least occasionally.

I see another factor in place which conflicts with our desire to get through to each other: We have to fight for survival in an increasing avalanche of incoming information…and for sanity's sake, we have to block out most of it. **Question: When people around us have a desperate need to get through to us, and we have a desperate need to block out most incoming information, what happens?**

With so many of us feeling numb, overloaded and unable to get through to each other, it takes more and more stimulation and sensationalism to penetrate the numbness. Yet as the stimulation and sensationalism increase, our numbness has to increase. Then the increasing numbness distorts and slows down our sorting and filing of information. Our confusion increases along with our worries that crucial information is misfiled or completely blocked out.

When we know our information-gathering and sorting process is impaired, we're afraid we can't trust ourselves and our perceptions and conclusions. So we're more uncomfortable than ever with our guesses. **It's easy to see that we go from our misperceptions to justifying anger and power struggles, and then the anger and power struggles further distort our perceptions and conclusions. What follows is an increasing loss of confidence in ourselves.**

☐ As we become more uneasy with ourselves, and more suspicious of others (who are also floundering around), we keep justifying our anger and getting it out, as that seems the thing to do. But we can't miss seeing that anger is contagious.

☐ In a climate of so much criticism and judgmentalism, we're destroying each other as problem solvers...at a time when we need each other the most. Whether we're talking about large-scale problems or small, in the present climate, who will "stick their necks out" to work on common problems? What appears to be happening is that we're seeing **a pool of finger pointers rising faster than the pool of effective problem solvers.**

☐ As problems multiply around us, can we stay numb enough, or hide enough, to be safe? Can we play Follow the Leader **enough** that we ourselves won't have to do anything to avoid the approaching fire-storm? Is there **enough** law enforcement available, anywhere, to protect us? In California, if the prison population increases at the present rate, before too many years, more than fifty percent of the residents will be in prison. **Question:** Will we be any safer then? or will we have to make it seventy-five percent? Will going in that direction make us safer? **Or, to survive, are we going to have to reverse this direction?**

The hope I see comes from thinking of all of us as problem solvers, every day, all day, as we're just trying to keep mentally and physically balanced. It's obvious to me that we desperately need to support each other in our struggles, and I especially mean the struggles to make sense of what's going on...so we can keep our heads up as much as possible.

And the way we support each other, I believe, is by listening, **listening.** That's what

I see that helps us, tremendously, as we're struggling.

When we talk to ourselves too much, it's easy to bend the truth...then maybe we'll wonder why our thoughts keep circling around instead of settling down. If we're talking to a listener, however, we're more obligated to straighten out our thoughts... and they'll lie down more quietly.

The hope I see is that something as small as listening, just a few more minutes each day, is the kind of thing we all can do. When we don't have to fight **quite so hard** to get through to each other, tension goes down. **This is a crucial direction change.**

Evidently Nero fiddled while Rome burned. And we can choose to fiddle too. But if we don't like being helpless, we can remember that many a crisis has been weathered by people repeating this ancient Chinese proverb: "It's better to light a candle than to curse the darkness."

(The following supplements are from earlier writings, some written with Pat Rooney.)

Supplement #1

Some suggestions
for getting through without anger

1.   **It's important** to prepare ourselves before trying to get through to another to get a fair hearing. This means giving ourselves a "ten" rating (on a scale of 1 to 10, that's the top) and holding onto it.

2.   **Be aware** that many people are naturally defensive (afraid of hearing something which might make them look bad in their own or others' eyes). Since it is to our advantage that others are willing to talk to us, we need to compensate for their defensiveness by showing appreciation by keen listening.

3.   **It's good** to remind ourselves that others aren't **automatically obligated** to listen just because we want to talk. (Nor are they obligated to talk just because we want information ... or we're bored.)

4.   **It helps** to be aware that **every time** we talk we are breaking into another's train of thought. We need to have a sense that our tidbits are from the sidelines, as the others' **processing their own information** is the main event...**for them.**

5.   **Listening**, even **overlistening**, comes ahead of trying to get through. We need to have some idea of what we're feeding into, what's going on with the other. (Usually, if we listen closely enough, we hear this message: "Appreciate me.")

6.   **When we care** to hear another person's feelings, it helps if we respond to show we have truly heard. Maybe we can say, "Sounds like you're feeling scared." (Or "hurt," or "desperate," whatever seems appropriate.) **Real hearing is a precious gift we can give each other.**

7. We are not ready to try to get through until we check with the other for willingness to listen. "**I've got some ideas about this, but I need to know if this is a good time to put them out...**"(Nothing is more futile than talking if another doesn't choose to hear: "You listen"..."Now you listen to me"..."No, no **you** listen to **me**.")

8. It's easiest to tell others how we feel if we are clear ourselves. It also helps to be able to keep our balance if we are continually aware of our feelings. Maybe we can describe them to ourselves by starting with physical feelings, as this may lead to awareness of deeper feelings. "I'm tense in my shoulders...Maybe I'm pushing too hard...I'm scared, trying too hard...pushing ... afraid I won't make it."

9. When practicing telling others our feelings, it helps to start with minor ones first: "I feel kind of uneasy tonight." Don't be surprised if the other wants to know why you feel as you do, or wants to help you change the feeling. But you don't have to get trapped into trying to explain while the other judges if your feelings are "right" for you or not. Your feelings are **always right for you.** You can simply say, "All I know is that's what I'm feeling now, and I just wanted to tell you about it."

10. To break a two-person communication jam, sometimes it helps to try **monologues.** One person talks until he or she chooses to stop, while the other takes notes. Then each switches parts, going back and forth, always waiting for the other to make a complete statement and be ready to listen before switching.

11. To minimize defensiveness in the listener, it helps to speak for ourselves:

> "I realize doing things your way is important to you and I can't expect you to be different...But I wouldn't feel right about myself if I didn't try to tell you how I feel. You wouldn't know unless I tell you, so I'm trying...**for my own reasons.** I'm working on the problem and I'm not sure yet what I'm going to do. But I wanted to let you know what's going on with me."

12. **Instead of trying** to impress others with our brilliant conversation, I like to remember a Portuguese saying that I consider to be the ultimate compliment: **"I like myself when I'm with you."**

13. **In writing long notes** in an effort to break a communication jam, here are two suggestions:

> ❖ One person writes a note and the other responds in writing, back and forth. Maybe a notebook can be kept in a certain drawer where each can look for responses.

> ❖ Both write long notes, separately, on the same subject, exchanging notes and going back and forth.

14. **Persistence** is probably the main key to getting through. If we aren't heaping blame on those who don't hear us, they may be the ones to coach us on how we might get through. I believe we need to practice getting through **every day.**

15. **Here's one definition of a friend:** One who cares enough to give us feedback in a way we can take.

16. **I suggest you ask questions very, very sparingly.** This last suggestion is so important (yet seems so little understood) that I'm going to devote extra space to it. (Some American Indians go so far as to say that if we have to ask questions we aren't ready to understand the answers.)

Of course our own questions seem harmless to us. But it's easy to forget that most of us, to some degree, live with the perpetual fear of being caught off guard, maybe feeling inadequate, looking stupid...like a "bad guy."

In our society, whenever we're asked questions, in order to be a "good guy" we're expected to respond (and maybe even be clever or helpful).

Probably you've had the experience of listening to questions and muttering to yourself, "What are they driving at?" Or if you've tried to answer you might have gotten this response, "No, no, that's not what I mean… what I want to know is…"

We'll say someone hastily asks you, "What'll I fix for dinner?" Maybe you'll give a stumbling answer which will irritate the questioner (whose thinking has probably already covered numerous possibilities). Then you might become irritated because you'd been asked the question in the first place.

It's easy to see that the other person would have been much more considerate of you if he/she had either 1) not asked the question at all, or 2) at the very least, revealed more of their train of thought **before** asking you to jump on the train:

"I'm trying to decide if I need to go to the store or not …or if I'll just fix _____ but that might take too long as Sally has to leave by 7 o'clock …so maybe I'd better…"

It's true that your hearing such a rambling statement might have been an unwelcome intrusion on your thoughts. But at least you'd have been spared the irritations which might have followed your stumbling response to the "What'll I fix for dinner" question.

When times are good, avoiding such irritations (whether you're asking questions or trying to respond) might not seem too important. **But in times of stress, even one unnecessary irritation can be too much.**

To break a questioning habit, probably at first all you can do, **after** you've asked a question, is to think of a statement you might have made instead. I predict that you'll be amazed how soon you'll see results **if even occasionally** you'll remember to avoid asking a question. You'll probably find yourself getting **different** information, and more of it…and I suspect it will be **much more valuable**…because it's willingly given. ☐

Supplement #2

Some questions
asked at seminars and workshops

Q: Wouldn't you be mad if someone cut in front of you on the freeway and nearly caused an accident?

A: No, because I don't have the anger habit. In fact, when I'm in a crisis, my head is never clearer. I need all the wits I've got and I don't want them distorted with anger. (What helped me most to break the habit was remembering that I couldn't be angry unless I was telling myself things which weren't true, lies, **ought to bes.** Every time I'd get angry, I'd remember this faster ... until eventually the downtime of my anger was practically nothing.)

Q: Don't you believe that anger is a good motivator to get us to do something we wouldn't do otherwise?

A: Maybe so, but I think we'd probably be doing the wrong things, things that would hurt us in the long run. No matter how pure our motives, I think if we analyze a situation and act out of anger, we'd be triggering polarization and resistance instead of cooperation.

Q: Can't all this be taught in schools?

A: I can't see why not, and the sooner the better.

Q: Wouldn't it be dull without anger?

A: I think it's the opposite. It's as if all doors are open wider ... and just living every day is more and more exciting.

Q: Isn't it all right to believe we're doing the best we can only most of the time?

A: No, as it's like accepting the baby only if his or her diapers are clean. It's the whole package we want acceptance for, and that's so hard to give. Laying our non-acceptance on others is the way we hurt them, and all we do is get the worst out of them.

Q: What do you do when someone is expressing anger at you?

A: I breathe deeply and remember that I'm all right. (Remember the "bad guy" doesn't live with me anymore.) So I just listen and stay out of the way. I know the other wants to get through, as maybe he or she is saying, "I'm desperate … no one really hears me…" I'd say absolutely nothing while the anger is high and maybe not for some time later. Because I've listened so closely, whatever response I'll make will come after making the best possible observations of the entire situation.

Q: What's the difference between the other books BREAK THE ANGER TRAP, THE ANGER PUZZLE, SHAKE THE ANGER HABIT! and now this one?

A: Naturally Pat and I always think the newest one is best. There's some overlap in all four books, but each one hits the subject from a different angle. It's my guess that you'll find plenty in the others to compensate for the overlap.

Q: Why do you think society made such a wrong turn and became obsessed with how we get anger out instead of looking at the way it's formed?

A: We've obviously known for a long time that talking had some connection with feeling better after getting angry. But instead of recognizing that it probably was the getting through (maybe later to a sympathetic third person) which was soothing to ruffled feathers, it was easy to jump to the conclusion that relieving the tension temporarily was all that was needed.

It's as if we thought that anger was hot air which needed releasing, and some counselors still goad their clients into getting their anger out. (Particularly for depressed people, this appears to bring them back to life, at least temporarily, and I know many counselors believe that it's impossible to be depressed and angry at the same time. See pages 89-90 of **SHAKE THE ANGER HABIT** and also **THE ANGER PUZZLE,** page 89, for my comments on this.)

In a counseling session I listen to **whatever** my clients want to say, and no time is spent specifically getting anger out. Why? I've learned that **when clients learn to stop forming anger today, their problems with anger disappear. Old buried anger is no longer a problem.** (The mindset which instantly "justified" anger is broken.)

So it's true that talking is related to easing anger. But from the way I see the entire picture, it's learning to talk more effectively which makes anger (and venting it) unnecessary.

Q: What's the best thing for you personally about being mostly without anger?

A: It's that people are willing to come close, and I'm getting tremendous amounts of information in addition to the good feelings which come with closeness. I love that. Before I became aware of all this, I kept seeing that people were backing away from me, yet it was so subtle that I couldn't put my hand on what was wrong. This kept the old bad-guy-something's-wrong-with-me feelings close to the surface.

Now I've listened long enough (and evidently made good enough observations) that I've found out how to live my own life enjoyably. You can probably imagine my pleasure to find that not only does all this work for me, but according to the feedback Pat and I are getting, it works for countless others too. No wonder we're celebrating!

What's extremely interesting to me is that Pat and I have traveled two completely different paths. From childhood he believed he could "make it" by being a pleaser (usually trying to please a strong woman), and I very early found that I couldn't please (so I became more independent in order to cover up the fact that I didn't know how to get cooperation).

How amazing that what makes life better for both of us is the same thing: daily practice in getting through (as often as possible) without anger. □

Supplement #3
A Road Map

I wrote this material originally to give to my clients so we wouldn't have to spend counseling time with he-did-this's and she-did-that's. And it worked. Since the first client who read it described is as a "road map," that name has stuck.

You may wonder why it seems so important to offer a description of a marriage going downhill. But then you remember that when you yourself get a chance to see a whole map spread out at once, you usually find routes you don't expect. The opposite, as you can guess, might be wandering around lost, yet not even knowing there's a map to check.

The Trip Down

The first sign that the "honeymoon is over" occurs when partners notice that their needs aren't met as fully as they once were.

It seems natural, when needs aren't filled the way one expects, to blame the person not filling the needs: the partner, of course.

Blaming, even if unexpressed directly, probably causes the partner to be less able and willing to do the expected need-filling.

Anger, whether open or denied, usually covers the hurts at the increasingly unfilled needs.

A kind of low-key power struggle begins in which each, probably in an indirect way, is trying to force the other to fill needs as before. Who starts the process doesn't really matter.

The methods used in attempts to make things better often **perpetuate problems** instead of solving them.

> ❖ A wife may talk little to her husband because she wants to avoid arguments. Her husband, desperate for more communication, shouts and storms (overdoing it, no doubt) to provoke responsiveness. The wife's attempt to prevent

arguments makes her "tune him out," blocking communication. The behavior of both, in attempting to make things better, actually makes them worse.

When problems seem to resist solution, each naturally wants to try harder (and more often) to make things better. But the trying usually means merely adding new twists to the same methods which are perpetuating the problem.

Discomfort increases as basic needs for respect, security and emotional support are threatened more often, due to the trying harder. And the added amounts of disappointment, hurt, anger and blaming further reduce accurate communication.

In the absence of accurate communication, unflattering interpretations of the other's behavior fill the vacuum.

> ❖ A wife believes her husband's silence is punishment for her when actually the silence may be due to hurt over previous attempts to communicate.

Unflattering interpretations of behavior justify and intensify the blaming of the other. The downhill slide of repeating patterns becomes even harder to reverse.

Misinterpretations of behavior mean that even a spouse's desired behavior may not make things better (the damned-if-I-do, damned-if-I-don't pattern).

> ❖ A wife begs her husband to stay home. He feels trapped and leaves, feeling guilty. When he later wants the security of home and returns, his wife believes it's only out of guilt, and not because he wants to, so she makes their time together miserable. Naturally the husband feels insecure and inadequate as a wife pleaser (whether he's away or at home) and the wife feels rejected and insecure (also whether he's away or at home), so a repeat of the pattern is assured.

Unawareness of one's misinterpretations about the other means that correcting distortions is impossible. Why should partners ask, and really want an answer to the question "What's going on with you?" when they already "know" the answer?

❖ A wife with preschool children is home, feeling trapped each day. She describes her husband as perfectly happy. "Why shouldn't he be happy? He's got everything he wants, freedom to run around all the time."

Her husband, uncomfortable at home with his family, yet not wanting to be "out in the cold," is completely miserable. He describes his wife, "Oh, she's happy all right. She's got the kids and the house."

With so many obstacles (increasing pain, fear, insecurity) to accurate perceptions, most ways of problem solving available to others go unseen and untried.

❖ A husband threatens to leave every time there's an argument, so the wife believes she'd better become more independent. Her husband sees her moves toward independence and feels their relationship is threatened so he tries to thwart her. Such thwarting makes her pursue her plan to become independent more intensely, which triggers more intense thwarting behavior.

(What's impossible for each partner to see, when the downhill slide has gained such momentum, is that each person triggers the other's behavior which perpetuates the pattern. It's nearly impossible, then, for them to assure each other that they want to continue the relationship, thereby easing the insecurity of each and reversing the pattern.)

Hopelessness becomes a heavy burden as the weight of the downhill slide makes it appear that partners have tried everything, and nothing is ever going to work. As long as the primary goal of each is to force a partner to become a better need-filler, the power struggle can never end.

But the power struggle will give way at some point to a goal of personal survival, as partners eventually find they must put all of their energy into trying to feel good enough about themselves in order to be able to cope with minimum requirements of survival. Any need-filling requests by the other, at this point, appear to be giant-sized, intolerable burdens. (This is usually the stage when one or the other moves out. Also suicide attempts or serious accidents sometimes occur at this point, as one partner makes a final desperate attempt to force the other to fill his/her needs.)

Survival behavior in one's self, naturally, seems different from that of the spouse (who, in the other's mind, at least, is really mostly happy). When one is asking shrilly, out of pain and anger, "Why did you do this to me?" the answer, "I did it simply to survive," can't even be uttered, much less heard.

During this phase, one person may be feeling that he/she is totally wrong and the other is totally right. (Others often reinforce this view. The partner who cares for small children is usually seen as good, for example, and anyone can tell that the spouse "out running around" is bad.) If a spouse accepts an angry partner's evaluation of him/her as a total failure as a need-filler, hence a failure as a person, there would be the possibility of suicide. No one can carry such total guilt for long: "I'm responsible for all our misery, and if I could just be different, everything would be all right." But with "being different" his/her only hope, and promises to "be good" nearly impossible to keep without awareness of the pattern the two of them are in, he/she is at a dead-end.

To resume pursuing even minimal survival activities, both must eventually conclude that he/she is mostly good, and it must be the partner who's bad. Unbearable fear that the opposite may be true must be squelched, maybe by anger.

Numbness may have taken over long before this point as a way of getting relief from too much hurt. But lessening one's sensitivity is self-defeating as it makes giving and receiving accurate information even more difficult.

Out of feelings such as numbness, helplessness and hopelessness, partners may strike out, possibly blindly, in attempts to feel better about themselves by demonstrating a capacity for violence or seeking other partners. But negative feelings, such as guilt and rejection, can hardly be avoided.

When partners discover that with a new person they can feel a little better about themselves, they often feel strong enough (and less forced to spend so much of their energy on survival) that they can try again with the original partner.

But confusion occurs at reconciliation attempts as the old repeating patterns resist good-intentioned tampering. A dead-end is reached when each finally accepts the fact that he/she has no possible power to change the other, yet the bad partner, the one who obviously must change in order to make things better, simply isn't ever going to change.

Counseling? "I want to go but my partner doesn't." The underlying message still is, "I'm good, and he/she's bad. He/she, the villain, isn't even willing to try." The partner's unspoken response is probably, "It would only take one more failure to put me under for good, and I'm just not going to risk it."

The final, "this time for good" break-up occurs when at least one partner simply can't feel good enough about him/herself in the relationship any longer. The ratio of bad feelings to good has finally become completely intolerable.

The Turn-Around and
the Road Uphill

Finding an uphill path won't occur until partners are far enough beyond the survival stage that they don't spend all their energy defending themselves and blaming the other. Because they aren't in as much pain, and therefore so intensely afraid of hearing even a hint of criticism, they can begin to hear others again. In this stage of openness, they may be able to learn from a marriage counselor, or by reading, or even listening a little differently to their same friends.

Progress occurs when partners can begin to hear each other's feelings more deeply. All each may hear at first is a little of the other's pain and survival struggle. But since each can identify with the same feelings, a bond flickers between them.

From that faint flicker, partners can begin to perceive each other a little more accurately. They then find it easier to accept the limitedness of the other's need-filling ability. This acceptance alone eliminates a major source of anger and blaming, and of course the reactions to such anger and blaming.

After a little time (with more hope present all the way) each can hear the other's expressions of feelings more often, and each can make responses to show such hearing. Just one time when a formerly habitually-angry spouse listens sympathetically and says, "Sounds like you're really feeling hurt (sad, scared, or whatever is appropriate)," the other will probably feel a surge of joy and even more hope.

When the climate is established in which each really cares, even occasionally, to hear the other deeply (and neither rushes in to try to change the other's feelings), both experience the excitement of increased hope.

At some point each person realizes he/she must accept responsibility for taking the initiative for feeling good and getting his/her own needs filled. This means that for both, long-carried burdens, the assumed responsibilities for the other's needs and feelings, are lifted. And each, even halfway, no longer needs to accept blame for not perceiving and filling the other's needs.

When partners have less need to be defensive (they're not feeling blamed, inadequate and insecure), they can hear more and more. And each can see more clearly his/her own part in any interchange, especially how his/her own responses perpetuate, or end, a circular pattern. (He/she can choose, for example, to nourish security in his/her partner rather than insecurity.)

When both feel better about themselves, at least part of the time, they are able to willingly give their partners emotional support. (This is, of course, the same emotional support each was formerly trying to force from the other.)

The basic communication needed for day-to-day problem solving, so difficult during the downhill spin, is at least possible now. Each has the skills to know how to get the best, instead of the worst, from the other.

There's no more helplessness, only choices whether or not to use new skills.

True marriage insurance is a feeling, the feeling that exists when each gives the other deep respect, the kind that becomes emotional support. Then each can say to the other, "I feel good about **myself** when we're together." Protected by the comfort and security of such insurance, each can probably look back and see clearly: Greediness and manipulations to get more from a partner than he/she is willing or able to give, followed by disappointment and lack of acceptance of him/her as a need-filler, lead to marriage instability. But cultivation and maintenance of communication skills, which lead to respect for a partner and his/her feelings (emotional support), develops true marriage insurance, the kind that can withstand maximum stress. □

Supplement #4

Comments on angry pleasers (those whose lives are controlled by fear of others' anger)...

What I've written here is a detailed description of the way a compulsive pleaser gets trapped in an increasingly painful lifestyle. (The more accurately a problem can be described, I believe, the more likely it can be eased.)

The term "angry pleaser" is used because it's my observation that angry people are those who continue to believe they ought to be able to please others and avoid any possible anger; then they get angry and blame themselves (or others) for their inevitable failures; and in the increasing pain of an angry lifestyle, they stay trapped by their inability to see that it's the way they're defining problems which keeps them insoluable.

I   What's Wrong

If you're a compulsive pleaser you're angry much of the time...

And you never can quite understand why your attempts to please don't get the results you expect.

> *"What's wrong?... What's wrong?... I was just trying to help... Why is everybody always jumping down my throat?"*

In your constant search to understand how to make things better, you're testing first one theory and then another: *"If only somebody would do this... or if only I could do that... or if only... if only... if only..."*

But your best theories never quite get you what you expect. And you really don't think you want too much: Just a little cooperation, even occasionally, or at least a tiny bit of appreciation... *"Nobody knows how hard I try."*

But you can't figure out what you're doing wrong. Surely you've got the power to make things better, haven't you? You'll just have to try harder... and harder... and harder...

II Something's Wrong with Me

Because you so often fail at getting what you want (respect, understanding, cooperation) you become increasingly afraid there's something wrong with you, something missing inside you.

Believing this helps you understand why you keep getting criticism for your best efforts.

In whatever way you define what's missing inside you, you ought to be able to figure out how to fill that empty space, shouldn't you? And then you could correct what's wrong, couldn't you?

Surely someday you'll be able to measure up, be where you want to be, "up to snuff." But it's not easy to fight something so vague. All you know for sure is that **it feels like there's a gap between where you are now and where you think you ought to be.**

This is so scary you need to prove to yourself (and everybody else if possible) that there's nothing wrong with you. You'll have to show you're above reproach, actually one of the good guys of the world.

The surest way to look good (to yourself at least) is to find opportunities for good deeds. Your helpfulness always gives you relief (if only temporary) from your fears of badness (inadequacy, being a nobody, or maybe just falling apart because of that missing space inside you).

It doesn't matter too much that your offering to help others may be irritating to them (as you're often implying that they can't do things right, your way). *"Here, use this knife to slice the tomatoes... it's better than that one..."*

What matters far more to you is that you can feel secure in the belief that you're being helpful. You live by the theory that if you do enough good deeds you'll feel better about yourself and others will see your true worth. You've believed this for so long it never occurs to you to test the theory. But then it's never needed testing. It's been too easy to explain each failure: *"If I'd just tried harder (been good enough) I'd have made it."*

Feeling helpless would be intolerable. You can't consider the possibility that you might be incapable of making things better... someday.

But believing you continually need to try harder means that you can't slow down, whether in sickness or in health. You might "lose ground," or "lose your grip." Then your painful feelings of emptiness might rush out and overwhelm you.

So you keep moving faster and faster, hanging even more tightly to the hope that things will have to get better... if you'll just try hard enough. But things aren't getting better, and you're repeatedly left with the only conclusion which makes sense to you: "There's got to be something wrong with me."

III The Search for Assurance

To continue to believe you have the power to make things better for yourself, you search even more diligently for proof of others' appreciation, acceptance, caring, cooperation, understanding...

You're busy evaluating what you're getting ("taking things personally"), and you can't seem to get quite enough of what you seek. *"Yes, they care for me, all right, but if they cared **enough**, they would..."*

Your constant search for that last drop of appreciation is risky because you're reading an evaluation of yourself into everything that happens: *"Am I getting what I deserve for what I do?"* Each time your answer is "no" you conclude you ought to be hurt. Then all your questions which follow lead nowhere: *"Am I really that bad?... Why do they do this to me?"*

Actually there's no way you can miss finding rejection as it's always out there, somewhere. Because your style is to "take things personally," finding any rejection at all is too much for you. You feel fragile, anyway, as if you're a house built of cards. It takes just removing one card (feeling one rejection) to bring the whole house crashing down.

> *"I was in the supermarket and I saw my best friend come in. And she actually turned the other way instead of coming over to talk to me as she usually does. It just kills me to have her treat me this way. All week I've gone over everything that happened when we were together last, and I just can't understand it. There's no reason for her to treat me like that." (Fact: The friend was having problems at home and was frantically trying to decide what to do. The last thing she could handle, just then, would have been trying to explain to someone else something she hadn't sorted out herself.)*

You continue to feel the rejection you despise so much because even those closest to you can't "bend over backwards" **enough**, or "go out of their way" **enough** so you can feel appreciated **enough**. (Because the first priority of all of us is keeping our own balance, in our own way, no matter how strange it may look to others, we're all extremely limited in how much we can help each other.)

But you're hurting (from the rejections) so you're searching harder and harder for evidence of appreciation in order to ease your hurts. Even though you believe you're hiding your disappointment in others (who aren't appreciating you enough) they most likely perceive it. **And they tend to feel inadequate around you, maybe**

guilty that they don't have more to give, or maybe resentful that they "owe" you for doing things they never asked you to do.

So what do they do? They get away if they can and try to find some place where they can feel better about themselves.

You're left confused and alone, repeatedly asking yourself the same questions.

> *"After all I've done for them, why are they leaving me?*
>
> *"What am I doing wrong? Don't they care they're making my life harder?*
>
> *"I never try to hurt anyone, why do they do this to me?*
>
> *"I want them to care enough to want to help me... why can't they do something for me just because they want to?"*

You search harder than ever for evidence that you're all right. Your only real comfort is the hope that you're capable of understanding what's going on... someday.

But sometimes you get so scared. What if the day is coming when you've tried everything you can think of? What if you really will be in a blind alley someday with nowhere to turn? **What if you never figure out how to be happy?**

All you know is that you can't stop trying to make things better. You can't take time out to lick your wounds. You absolutely have to search even more diligently for something else to try. Yes, someday, you'll find respect, closeness... happiness.

IV Who's to Blame

It seems as if you could get relief from your increasing pain if you could just know (for sure) who or what to blame. Then surely you'd know (for sure) what you ought to be trying next.

To cope with your ever-present fear that you're not good enough, coupled always with your desperate need to believe the opposite, you're diligent in finding evidence so you can justify blaming others for your troubles. And you don't mind looking to the past, present and future.

Armed with plenty of evidence of others' badness, you can keep letting them know how wrong they are so they'll change and things can get better for you. (Then you'll feel powerful, able to make things better, not helpless after all.)

You'll do whatever you need to do (and think whatever you need to think) as long as you can shift the blame away from yourself.

At least you can't feel helpless (or worthless). You can keep busy letting others know, maybe more and more forcefully, what you think they ought to be doing. Then they'll have to see things your way.

But it's hard to keep believing you're making things better when you're constantly triggering retaliation.

Because others don't enjoy assuming the position of villains around you **(just because they aren't doing what you think they ought to be doing so you can feel better about yourself)** they're confused and unhappy. And usually they're willing to let you know it.

Retaliation can be dangerous for many reasons, but the worst for you is that **it triggers your most painful fear: that maybe it really is your own badness that's the problem**.

Yet, as with any kind of blaming, it doesn't really help the problem. **But you have to keep trying to make things better, don't you? If you quit trying you might as well be dead**.

Whenever the thought tries to surface that you yourself might be to blame, you have to dismiss it. The terror is too great to bear that you might not be doing the right things... **when you're trying night and day to find out what the right things are**.

In order to avoid such terror you have to focus **nearly every second** on trying to convince yourself and others that they are the ones causing your problems.

But you pay a heavy price for this lifestyle, as it means going around in circles. Your blaming others leads to their retaliation... to more blaming... to more retaliation...

V   Being Nice Is Better Than Getting Angry

But how can you get cooperation? How can you get help when you need it? How can you get others to stay close by? How can you feel better? **Will you ever be happy?**

You know you'd rather be nice than angry. You like it when others smile at you and want to be close, as then maybe you'll get some cooperation and your life will be easier.

But even when you try so hard to be nice, sometimes your anger comes out against your will. If you feel wronged enough, you may explode: *"You're a stupid jerk... it's your fault that things are all messed up... I'm sick and tired of what you're doing..."*

Although you'd like to believe things will get better after your outburst, they actually get worse. Those you've yelled at may conclude that you're the one who's the jerk. **And you probably triggered their own guilt, their fears of being bad, wrong. So they either want to fight you... or stay away.**

But you have to believe that anytime you get angry it must be others' fault. *"If only they'd do what I want, I wouldn't have to scream at them... (and then I could be nice, the way I'm trying to be...)."*

Whenever your anger breaks loose (and shocks you

as much as others) it doesn't mean you've lost faith in the power of your niceness. **No one regrets that you lost your temper any more than you (contrary to what bystanders may think)**.

Each time you get angry it's because you feel helpless and desperately disappointed that the power of your niceness isn't enough to get what you want.

But you know your anger pushes others away. So what can you do? **Be nicer, of course**. You find yourself continually making vows to try harder to be nice. Surely, **if you try hard enough**, you can keep from blowing up and ruining everything.

But it's confusing when sometimes your anger comes out and it feels good. You get a burst of relief from physical tension and also a surge of power (even if brief). That power is especially welcome because it banishes fears of your helplessness.

You want very much to believe that your anger will get you what you want... once and for all, and then you won't have to get angry again. But your anger never gets you what you expect... once and for all... **even when others meet your demands.**

> *"My guitar was destroyed in a house fire and all I could do was complain to my partner. Every day, complain, complain. So he finally went out and bought me a new guitar, but he spent more than we could afford. So I felt guilty, then worse and worse. It got so bad I couldn't enjoy playing the guitar at all. (But things got worse when my partner got mad at me. He took it as a personal insult that I didn't appreciate his gift.)"*

For one thing, when you're controlling others with your anger, you can't ever tell whether they're doing what you want because they care for you... or because they fear your anger.

And no matter how another responds to your anger,

you can't really know the damage you do.

But one reason your outburst doesn't get what you want is that you may feel so embarrassed and ashamed of your anger (in such a nice guy as you) that you apologize immediately. ("I didn't mean it... I'm just having a bad day...") Then you've nullified any chance of getting even temporary changes from others (even if grudgingly given).

But what's worse is that you know from experience that your anger hurts you, especially in the long run. Yet you keep finding yourself angry, again and again. And you know you're building higher hurdles between you and your real goals (closeness, cooperation, caring...).

Whenever you "tell off" others you get a predictable result:

> Either you reap instant rebellion (even if silent) and more resistance to the changes you've been seeking by your niceness...

> Or you get instant compliance (from another pleaser). Since in the long run such pleasers will pull away from you, your "telling off" another isn't helping you at all, unless your goal is to be isolated.

You hate so much to be isolated by your anger you continue to believe you have just one choice: be nicer.

VI The Need to Avoid Feedback

Because you already hurt so much (at failing to get what you want either by your niceness or anger) you have to avoid feedback at all costs. (You never know in advance what you'll hear, and there's always criticism lurking out there, somewhere, ready to disgrace you in an unguarded moment.)

So you find yourself incessantly defending your helping/pleasing lifestyle to yourself and to others. **You'll tell**

yourself whatever is necessary to stay convinced that such a lifestyle is working for you.

You're becoming so vigilant in detecting possible criticism that every move you make is controlled by the need to avoid seeing even minor hints of others' disapproval.

But blocking feedback in order to avoid criticism means that you're trying to make things better without getting accurate information about what's going on around you.

Instead of making your life easier, it's the opposite. All your problem-solving is confused when it's based on your guesses about what's going on... and what you think ought to be going on.

You're becoming trapped inside your own head, left mostly with your own observations and your own ways of processing information. **This is a dangerous price to pay for your safety from criticism.**

Yet even in isolation it isn't always possible to believe that it's others who are causing your problems. The fear that you yourself might be bad is always just under the surface. What if you really aren't capable of making it?

Even asking the question causes terror, terror so great it propels you to break isolation and risk getting feedback once again. Surely you can show others how valuable you are and then you'll get the appreciation you deserve. *"Just tell me what I'm doing wrong and I'll correct it."*

But fresh from your isolation, you aren't able to see problems clearly and define them accurately. So it's inevitable that the ways you're choosing to make things better usually make them worse instead. The more you think you win, the more you actually lose. **You're in a pattern of trying harder and enjoying it less.**

Maybe you put all your energy on appearance, for example, so no one will suspect there's something wrong with you. *"If I can just look good enough, I'll be all right."*

But the contrast between how you look to others and what you feel inside gives you one more reason to feel bad. **It's as if you're not only feeling empty, wrong, inadequate, but you're also a fraud, hiding the truth from others.** So the more you believe you succeed at looking good, the greater is your pain because others don't know how to relate to you. Because they may perceive you as "having it all together" they don't believe you when you try to tell them it isn't true.

You may have a passion for order, whether in material things or people. It's terribly important to you that others see you as knowing how things ought to be. But this is exhausting for you and irritating to others. They continually resist your attempts to get them to help you keep everything and everybody shaped up. So the harder you try to make things better the more you get the opposite.

Maybe you exaggerate your achievements in your desperate need to feel important. But others may not respond with compassion because they may not realize you're trying to compensate for your fears of failure. **So they get irritated at your exaggerations and ignore you, and you feel less important than ever.**

Maybe you give presents you can't afford. But whenever you give to others out of your own need to be seen as a good guy, it's not surprising that the responses to your giving may be disappointing.

It's possible you believe the real cure for your troubles would be to find a partner who would appreciate you properly. So maybe you spend your energy searching repeatedly and in vain for that partner. But you'll probably intensify your niceness in an effort to hold onto a prospective partner, always expecting that your niceness can get that continuous stream of appreciation you crave.

But the prospective partners fear you'll expect more in return for such niceness than they can give. **So they pull away from you rather than stay and feel inadequate, never able to give you enough.**

You probably are constantly criticizing just about everything in an effort to raise yourself up a little. But those around you become uneasy when they wonder what you say about them behind their backs.

You constantly return for comfort to your all-time favorite way of showing you're above reproach (and can't possibly deserve anyone's anger, criticism, blaming). You can always do another good deed. Then it won't matter what's going on around you, as at least briefly you can convince yourself that you're more than just all right, you're actually a good guy. But when you do good deeds out of your need to be recognized and have impact, you may be overdoing it. **Then others may be forced to reject you in order to be safe from your interference in their lives.**

You've long believed that you have the power to know what others want... and that you're able to give it to them. **But to continue to believe this you have to be sure you hide the evidence of your failures... especially from yourself.**

So you're working every second at justifying your lifestyle to yourself, and you succeed, sometimes, at least from your own point of view. But being locked into the need for holding onto this safe point of view creates more problems. Others' feedback to you isn't making sense. You constantly find yourself saying, *"I can't understand... there's no reason for that... why?... why?... why?..."*

Any time there's a conflict between what another person says and your perceptions, you have to work hard to preserve your own version of the truth.

Other people may be trying in vain to get through to you, to help you understand why your lifestyle is hurting you so much. But sometimes, because they don't want to hurt you, they have trouble telling you the truth. For example, they probably don't want to say, *"You're driving me crazy when you do that."* Instead they might say, *"Don't bother."* And maybe you'll respond, *"Oh, it's no bother."* Then you continue to do what the other didn't want you to do in the first place.

But when others repeatedly can't get through to you in serious matters so you'll at least listen to their views, you're in real danger. It's when others become desperate enough in their failure to get through to someone that they may resort to violence.

But your lifestyle depends on staying inside your own world with your own point of view. That's the only way you can be safe and continue to believe that you truly are helping others. But you have to repeatedly explain to yourself that it's only because others are ungrateful that you don't get the rewards you deserve. Otherwise you'd have no explanation as to why others seem to be making your life harder.

But you're seriously handicapped in day-to-day problem-solving. You're trapped between the necessity for corrective feedback (to assure your own safety and survival) and the fear of getting it.

VII The Truth Gets Lost... Sometimes

You search to understand what's wrong (so you can make things better) but you're floundering because you can't get accurate feedback. But how can you get feedback when you're afraid of it? How can you know your effect on others? How can you know if you're expecting too much of yourself or others?

It's practically impossible for you to tell others the truth as you're so afraid of criticism: *"Oh no, let me do it... No, I don't mind... You go off and enjoy yourself."* You'll say nearly anything to avoid **even the possibility** of another's showing disappointment or irritation.

Maybe you tell yourself you can't tell the truth because you don't want to hurt anyone. But what you're probably doing is trying to avoid **seeing** any hurt feelings in another's eyes (**as that would be proof to you that you're really a bad guy in disguise**). *"I'd rather run and hide than see her cry. So I just say what I think she wants to hear... or else I avoid talking to her at all."*

Because you know that you're sometimes unable to tell the truth, you suspect that others may be the same way. And this realization makes you increasingly uncomfortable. How can you get along in a scary world if you can't tell what's going on?

Maybe you'll never find out how to be happy, and you'll just be miserable the rest of your life.

This thought is so frightening you've got to work harder to understand what's going on. But you may be getting the truth from others (especially pleasers) only when they're angry, after their nice-guy act has fallen apart. By then their feedback is just too harsh and you have to push it away. *"They're just mad because I'm not doing more... they never liked me anyway... they take me for granted, that's why they act like they don't appreciate what I do."*

It also makes it hard for you to understand what's going on when others are so embarrassed about their anger they instantly apologize. *"I didn't mean it... you know that..."*

Because you want so badly to believe they didn't mean it, that's what you choose to believe... to your own confusion.

The belief isn't comfortable as it conflicts too much with your own evidence. **You know that when you yourself are angry, you do mean what you say, at least for that minute.** Of course you may feel different later and regret what you said.

Even if you're uncomfortable in believing that others don't mean what they say in anger, you're forced to believe it. It's a necessity if you're to feel safe from your too-painful fears of badness.

Because your entire life is a struggle to understand what's going on so you can avoid others' anger, you

feel you have no choice but to be nicer... and nicer... and nicer.

So you continue trying to read minds in order to give others what you think they want. But you're continually surprised and hurt that you're getting so much criticism for your best efforts.

Even if it were possible for others to tell you what they want, and if it were possible for you to deliver it exactly, they still might blame you if they're not pleased. Your failure, in their eyes, would be that you didn't make them feel as good **as they expected**.

It's becoming increasingly evident that a lifestyle of trying to please others (so you can believe you're making them happy and you can feel like a good guy) keeps you in an impossible position. **It guarantees that much of the time you'll be failing and frantically trying to find out what's wrong. And to you, this means finding who or what to blame.**

But your blaming (whether it's self-anger or anger directed at others) keeps you caught in a circular trap of hurting more, trying more and failing more... then hurting/trying/failing... And you're no closer to understanding what's wrong or how to make things better.

When you find yourself overcommitted you can hardly face letting someone down (who might then think you're bad). So you may try to borrow strength from others: *"Will you stop by Joe's house... somebody's got to help him..."*

Because others resist your including them in your helping-pleasing lifestyle, they may get angry at you. But you get angry at them in return, as they're depriving you of the chance to be an even better guy (stronger and more powerful).

How can you ever get enough strength to make it when others won't help you? It isn't easy when others are hearing this confusing message: *"I'm so overwhelmed, nobody understands how hard I try... But let me do it all...*

I'm so eager to look like a good guy (and get a drop of appreciation) that I welcome the opportunity to do more."

No wonder others pull away in confusion and you're continually discouraged. But you're not a quitter. So you push on, telling all who will listen, "Here, let me help." But all the while your self-doubts come through, *"What if I'm doing everything wrong?"*

Most of your energy is going to guard the dark secret that you really are a bad guy because of all the stupid things you do. How can you live with the risk of exposing that bad guy hidden in there? It's like knowing there's a monster inside, always ready to jump out and embarrass you.

Because you can't admit your failures, limitations, errors or misjudgments (even to yourself) you're seriously handicapped in the way you relate to others. How can they know what's going on with you if you can't tell them?

Even when others treat you well or give you a compliment, you feel guilty and can't accept it. *"They just don't know what I'm really like."*

Others are increasingly uncomfortable with you because what you're saying isn't quite adding up.

VIII Nothing is Better

Those around you seem to be expecting you to do more and more and more. Because they may see you as strong (as you try so hard to show you are), they may be saying, "Oh, let him/her do it... He/she likes to do everything..."

Your confusing messages mean that your fantasy of getting help, of being rescued from your overcommitments, continues to be only a fantasy. **No matter how much you try to get help, you can't find enough to make you feel good.**

When bystanders see that you're exhausted and over-extended, they can't understand why you don't take their advice: *"You've got to stand up for yourself and say 'no' more often."* What they don't see is that you're incessantly looking for opportunities to do good deeds... for your own reasons (in order to avoid feeling like a bad guy).

So your short-term success is doing the deed... even if you have to ignore the response you get (maybe from both the recipient of the deed as well as bystanders).

One reason you hate to say "no" is that you identify with others who are hurting... all the time, as you're imagining that you understand how they feel. You long to ease their burdens. You know how much you yourself desperately crave help sometimes.

So you're constantly thinking of others. You want to be ready to help them, even if only to give good advice.

But you take it personally if the help/advice isn't taken. **It's as if each rejection means a step backward for you, just one more blow falling on your already-bruised head.**

You hate to say "no" to anyone asking for help. And when you do say "no" (and feel guilty), you blame the person who asked for help because you're feeling guilty.

In your confusion and pain, all you know for sure is that something is terribly, terribly wrong. And you feel like a failure more and more often.

No matter what the facts of any situation, you're probably muttering on and on and on: **"I couldn't let him fall on his face, could I?... I didn't want to see her disappointed... I didn't have any choice... I had to... She needs me... I was so tired I could hardly move..."**

You often feel that you're out of control, careening between one good deed and another. And you feel "caught in the middle" at times as you can't continually please two different people (and avoid their anger). But you have to believe it's their fault you're "caught in the middle."

Maybe you're following in the unhappy footsteps of someone you knew in childhood who would complain bitterly, *"You ungrateful wretches... I'm working my fingers to the bone for you... and the only reward I'll ever get will be in heaven."*

You're increasingly confused by the way others react to your blaming them for not helping you (to do what you're choosing to do). You have trouble understanding why they seem to blame you for everything that's wrong.

Since you've believed so long that **you** have the power to make others feel good (by your helping/pleasing) it's no wonder that **they too** expect you to make them happy. And if they aren't as happy as they think they ought to be, you tell yourself that it's your fault. **It's always easy to believe that you just aren't doing all you ought to be doing.**

IX Futile Power Struggles

But the tragedy of your lifestyle (of trying so hard to convince yourself you're good enough) is that it appears to others that you're always trying to be one-up, better than those around you.

This has a serious, unwanted side effect: Others believe you're seeing them as one-down and they don't like it. So they look for opportunities to "cut you down to size."

The problem comes from your belief that you can't just do what others do and feel good about yourself. For you it takes doing more, as you're trying to fill that missing space inside you, be "up to snuff" as you believe you ought to be.

Because others continually see you straining, striving and pushing, when they're around you they're conscious of feeling either up or down.

But the real problem is that it's unlikely you're aware of playing one-up, yet that's what makes others defensive around you. Because you're unaware of the cause of the damage you're doing, you're unable to correct it.

In your habitually helpful style you might be continually saying such things as this: *"Here, do it this way. Let me show you."* Often others see you as if you're assuming that you're the standard of the way things ought to be. *"I do this... you should too."*

Yet from your point of view you're only trying to get others (and yourself) to see how valuable you are.

But what's happening is that in your need to continually justify your lifestyle you don't realize how such justifications are sounding to others. What they hear is this: *"I'm always right... better than those around me."*

Your confusion is real when you get a glimpse of what others are thinking: *"Oh, he thinks he's perfect."* **Since you don't feel perfect... at all, you don't understand the criticism... at all.**

Others may perceive you as strong and independent, never suspecting that this is a pose you've forced yourself to accept... all because you've never been able to figure out how to get cooperation.

It's true, however, that sometimes the worse those around you look, the better you feel: *"At least I'm not doing that... and that... and that..."* But you have mixed feelings. You continually tell yourself that if others aren't happy around you it must be a reflection on you. So you vow to do the right things more and more often.

What you're missing, to your constant peril, is the awareness that you're in a world in which others also want to feel good about themselves. And they want to do it just as you do, by showing how capable they are. (The reason this is so hard for you to see is that when you take over, others probably back away.)

You're seriously handicapped in the way you relate to others when it's essential to you that you keep the one-up spot (even if you don't realize that's what you're doing). The only people who can be comfortable around you must be willing to play one-down. After so long, when they fully understand the role they are expected to play around you, they may either fight you for the one-up position... or they may get away (even if only mentally).

It's most likely that those around you at one time wanted nothing more than to please you. And as they leave, they probably are mumbling: *"I never could do enough..."*

In your incessant need to get assurance that you truly are all right, no one can give you enough appreciation. There isn't enough appreciation available, anywhere, to ease the pain of your helping/pleasing/one-up lifestyle.

When others try to explain how they feel around you, you still find it difficult to believe your overhelpfulness (over-niceness, over-protectiveness) is a put-down to them. But it's as if you're constantly saying to everyone who will listen:

> "I can do that... you can't."
>
> "I'm strong... you're weak."
>
> "Let me do everything... you'll probably mess up."
>
> "I'm smart... you're stupid."

Others may not realize how strongly you need to be constantly trying to help them (for your own reasons). **So they take your behavior to be an indication you continually see them as inadequate, bad, and just not what they ought to be.**

They feel guilty and confused. *"After all the help he/she's given me, why do I feel so terrible and always want to get away? I must really be the world's worst heel."*

It's difficult for you to see that your helpfulness is a constant put-down to others. So you continue to say to yourself, *"It surely can't be a crime to try to help, can it?"* **And you choose to believe it's virtuous to keep doing the same things.**

It would probably be inconceivable to you that just offering to help sometimes may be offensive, regardless of the facts of any situation. Your offer may just be an irritating reminder of your assumed one-up status, just one more of your continuing demonstrations that obviously you're in better shape than those around you, always able to lean over and help some peasant down below who just isn't up to your level.

Whatever is going on, you too find yourself defensive and confused: *"Since I was just trying to help, that can't possibly be bad. If you want to bite my head off, you must be the one who's bad."*

When two people are relating to each other in a one-up/one-down pattern, both usually can play both parts. But the one-down position is assumed unwillingly. So power struggles go on and on. *"I'm right, so obviously you must be wrong." "No, no, you're the one who's wrong..." "You're crazy"... "You're the one who's crazy..."*

Of course there's no winning. Even if the losers seem beaten down for good, they're really only biding their time, waiting for a chance to be one-up. It's a never-ending roller coaster, and no part of the ride feels good.

With two pleasers interacting (and all of us are pleasers to some extent) the possibilities for pain are endless. The more each person hurts, the more each person tends to play one-up (even if only mentally) in an attempt to feel better... and the more ugly the consequences.

In so much misery it's difficult for either of you to see how much you're alike. **You may be fooled by the fact that one of you is pushing, trying to make things better by doing more, and the other is withdrawing, trying to make things better by doing less.** Outsiders believe they know who is "right" or "wrong," but actually both of you are fighting to keep your balance in the only way you know. Look at the similarities:

> Neither of you feel as good about yourselves as you think you ought to.

> And both of you try desperately to avoid the other's anger.

> So you both are afraid to really listen to the other,

which means that neither of you feel you can get through to the other.

And both of you probably make things worse by blaming either yourself or the other.

Yet both of you are hungry for the same respect, appreciation, understanding, caring...

And both of you simply don't know how to get such good feelings.

Part of the time you both believe in the power of your niceness (as you know your anger doesn't work for you). But you get angry anyway, whether you believe you really ought to or because it comes out unbidden. But at times you hate yourself for being too nice.. and ineffective. "I really ought to put my foot down."

But you find, repeatedly, that when neither anger nor niceness gets you what you want, your confusion and pain and loneliness increase.

So you crave even more comfort, respect, understanding...

But you're feeling tremendously helpless most of the time, as such rewards seem constantly moving further out of your reach.

In your misery you each tend to see only your own pain. And you believe the other really ought to care enough to make your life easier. Both of you are saying to the other: *"You're not even trying to help me."*

X You Want Real Help

You know you long for help in finding a more comfortable lifestyle, but what kind of help do you need? and where to find it?

Your life becomes a search for the right kind of help, the

kind which fits you, the kind which will lead to your getting cooperation, appreciation, happiness...

Even if you were able to know exactly the kind of help you wanted, it wouldn't be possible to find anyone willing and able to give it when and how you want it. Yet when others' help doesn't seem to help, your tendency is to conclude it must be your fault, somehow, some way.

Maybe this is like being lost in a wilderness, on a wrong path, but convinced that if you'll just stay on the path long enough and try harder (be nicer to everyone you meet) you'll reach your destination.

But so far you haven't been able to take others' suggestions for finding a better path. Just seeking advice is hard enough, but rejecting it is even more painful. You have to see others' disappointment in you (whenever they feel your rejection). **So you're left feeling you must be worse than all others if you can't even take good advice (especially when it comes from someone who really cares for you, one who really wants to help you).**

Sometimes you feel obligated to take advice even if you've tried it before and know it won't work. Because you're hurting so much yourself, and can't bear to see the hurt in another's eyes at your rejection, you take the advice anyway. Yet you know you'll be the loser, just chalking up one more failure.

Maybe it's too uncomfortable to talk to others about what's really going on with you. To ask for help you'd have to risk revealing your failures, your feeling of emptiness. **Just being reminded of the deep gap between your good-guy appearance and what you really feel inside would mean abandoning your entire lifestyle (which has been based on avoiding seeing that gap).**

But sometimes you do talk to others when you're secure in the belief that they can't possibly suspect there's anything wrong with you. But you have to be on guard to keep the conversation superficial so you can avoid serious feedback.

You can't risk hearing anything from anyone who suspects what's really going on inside you.

Maybe at some point in your search for help you do find others who share similar experiences. Then you can talk and maybe listen, and at first it feels great to find out you're not alone. But you soon realize you may not be finding help in breaking the pattern you're in. **Others may still be lost in the same wilderness.**

It's possible you're one of those who can talk easily and incessantly about how wronged you've been, how bad others are and how helpless you are to make things better. Others probably pull away from you when they find there is no end to your story, just more details of the same plot.

Maybe you believe that getting your anger out will get rid of it. So you get it out. But the anger doesn't dissipate. In fact telling others of your troubles may attract allies, and you'll reinforce each other. You may get even angrier at those villains you believe are doing you wrong. **Or you may get angrier at yourself and feel even more guilty and helpless because you aren't making things better.**

It may be a relief if others leave you alone. You can't stand to hear, one more time, *"You've got to take responsibility for yourself... You've got to....."* Little do others know how hard you try... and try... and try.

Your only conclusion is that no one can possibly understand you. You must be totally different, wrong, bad. You're left more and more alone with your pain, alone and lost in a wilderness.

XI Time to Give Up?

At some point maybe you decide to quit trying so hard... then it won't hurt so much to fail. So you do nothing for awhile, just give up.

You've been increasingly isolated anyway, but now you're giving up your search for understanding. **If you'll just**

stumble along and make no decisions then maybe you'll be safe from criticism and pain. Maybe you can just play "Follow the Leader."

But others criticize you for making no decisions, and this reinforces your self-hate because you've given up.

In your isolation, even if it's of your own choosing, your pain is so great that sometimes you feel an overwhelming urge to find proof you're not totally bad. But every time you come out of isolation, you return to the trap of the same hurt-try-fail cycle. So you give up once more.

You may try suicide, **or just feel miserable over a period of many, many years.** Maybe all that changes at different times is the degree of misery.

To others your behavior may seem bizarre, as maybe all they can see is your anger alternated with your niceness. **They know they can't feel safe from your anger... or help you feel better.**

In this state of misery you'll do anything (however ridiculous and obnoxious) to keep others from moving away from you. But they move away just the same. So you get angrier and maybe try to force them to stay close. Then, as they inevitably have to get away, there's no one to comfort you in your pain.

You're now totally alone to deal with the consequences of your behavior. At last you're totally convinced that you're really the worst of all bad guys.

Probably the easiest way to avoid your unbearable pain is to go numb, turn yourself off and feel nothing. **No good feelings can get through your numbness, however, so you're paying an enormous price to avoid bad feelings.**

It's a real handicap to try to function without being aware of your feelings. You take what people say literally, as if you have to stay on the surface of every conversation, not get down where feelings might burst out. So you aren't in tune with where most people live, which is with their feelings. It's as if you're always out of touch, on the sidelines, alienated, alone in a world of your own.

Your problems are increasing whenever you're so numb you can't be sensitive either to your own feelings... or others'. **You have to live by your guesses of what you think you feel... and also what you think others feel. You're living without the most valuable tool for running your life, genuine sensitivity.** Because you have long thought you understood others' feelings, you've believed you were unusually sensitive. The belief in your unusual sensitivity is probably the explanation you're giving yourself for being a helper/pleaser. But this is the kind of one-up belief **(that others are insensitive as compared to you)** which infuriates them. Yet you need to keep the belief in order to account for the fact that others don't see things your way.

Without genuine sensitivity to your own feelings, your decisions about what you ought to be doing are more than ever off target. Less often are others hesitating to say to you, *"You're driving me crazy."*

In your numbness you try in vain to find something which will excite you, wake you up, make you feel good. But when you're so numb, nothing feels good. You find yourself sadly saying, *"I don't know what I want."*

Others may persist: *"Get out of my hair. Go find something of your own to do."* But you can't without feeling guilty that you're letting everyone down by not putting your energy into helping them.

You may have all kinds of health problems as your body is telling you that you can't go on. Maybe you feel pain in your chest, for example, as if you're holding your breath, afraid to breathe for fear of hurting someone. You may be telling yourself, *"That's all bad guys can do, hurt the ones they love."*

Fortunately, every time you need to feel better, even if only briefly, you can find someone to blame. *"It's my bad partner. If I can just leave him (her) I'll be all right."*

Whenever you hurt more than you can stand, you'll try any form of painkiller (legal or illegal), whatever the consequences. Maybe you'll live inside a fog of daydreams, or go anywhere or do anything to escape the too-great misery of your down-to-earth activities.

But this makes every necessary down-to-earth activity more difficult. So both your real and perceived failures are multiplying.

When you've withdrawn far enough from your misery that you believe you can stay safe from criticism and rejection, **maybe your anger is the only feeling strong enough to cut through your numbness. So you get angry in order to feel alive, have impact, feel important. You tell others how bad they are for not doing what you think they ought to be doing. Your hope is always that if you can just get angry enough (or show how hurt you are) others will change so you can feel better.**

But as always, your anger pushes others further away. They don't care to hear you just so you can feel more alive, feel that you have impact, that you're really not on the sidelines.

Because you still believe in the power of being nice (if you could just do it) your getting angry (no matter how justified it seems) is painful evidence you're just not good enough, not nice enough. In fact, there's no longer any doubt: you really are a bad guy.

At times, you even feel you might as well act like one and let everyone know how bad you really are. It's almost a relief after trying so long to be nice.

At last your helplessness is total. No matter what you do, or how much you hurt, you can't find how to get others to come close and comfort you.

How is it possible to get off such a path? I'll summarize the way I see the problem and I think you'll clearly see how a solution emerges.

Angry pleasers are those who 1) perceive themselves as bad and live in fear of others' anger (which would confirm their perceived badness); 2) so they reach the conclusion that they should spend all their energy proving that they're not bad after all; 3) but when they don't really believe that themselves, all their "proving" efforts are futile, and 4) in confusion and pain, they become stuck in compulsive behavior which not only is unrewarding to themselves but triggers anger in others; 5) so it seems that no matter what they do, they get the opposite of the closeness and comfort they want.

All it takes to get off the angry-pleaser path, the way I see it, is to realize that **we have a choice** about the way we see the world. If we want to, we can see a world in which **all of us** are doing the best we can, all the time, just trying to keep our balance. **Or we can choose to believe the opposite.**

I've tried to show in these pages the result of the latter choice.

Also, I thought you'd like to see, if you're an angry pleaser, that you weren't crazy for making the choices you did. Each one seemed totally logical, based on your starting place of not feeling good about yourself.

What helps me choose to believe that I'm doing the best I can all the time, just trying to keep my balance in ways no one else can ever understand, is this: I can never know, for sure, what is right for me at any one minute **until I try it. This means I'm certain it's impossible for anyone else to know.**

If others want to pretend they know, and get angry with me, it's apparent to me their anger is their own thing (and they're whirling inside their own anger trap).

I don't have to pass out when I'm the target of anger, and I don't ever have to hang my head and apologize for my "badness".... or make everything worse **for myself** by returning anger.

When we're no longer controlled by fear of others' disapproval/disappointment/anger, we're free to be working at keeping our own balance. And from that position our choices become better and better.

Of course we'll continue to choose to try to help each other, occasionally, and even try to please each other, occasionally. But we can also see that **our most valuable helping probably is indirect, maybe completely unexpected... and probably unconsciously given and maybe unconsciously received.**

The more we feel good about ourselves, the less the old-angry pleaser lifestyle can creep back to control us. It's as if continual focusing on keeping our own balance makes everything and every decision seem new... and exciting.

If we think of a baby's trying to learn to walk from watching others, we can see what's happening. There's no way we can learn to keep our balance except by finding the courage to risk trying the first baby steps.

Yet it's a risk-taking which never stops. We can fail at any time and maybe feel foolish, exposed as a bad guy, incompetent, a disgrace.

But it's only by taking the risks inherent in balancing that we can move ahead. The opposite is to be afraid to move for fear of incurring even the faintest possibility of anger, then compounding our problems by blaming others because we ourselves are afraid to move.

When we're not incessantly and blindly trying to get others' goodwill, it's as if we can open our eyes and see a world in which all of us are engrossed in the same scary balancing act. There's no one-up or one-down, just people struggling in different places and in different ways.

I see all of us as making decisions by processing our lifelong collection of bits and pieces of information, trying to decide what our next step should be. **It's as if, minute by minute, we're sorting through our private "garbage" heap.** Many of the fragments are barely recognizable, although sometimes we might glimpse a priceless jewel. (We'd probably like to think of our minds as full of neat rows of orderly thoughts. But I'm using the term "garbage" to imply that much of what comes into the pile is in unrelated segments, and they certainly don't all come by our choice.)

However we describe our process of decision making, it's clear that no one else could ever have access to all the pieces of our garbage heap, much less could anyone else be able to determine what our next step should be... or to take it. **So we're left essentially alone with the most important... and risky... job of our lives.**

And it's not easy to get much comfort from each other, as we can never explain what's going on with our garbage-sorting-decision-making at any one time. The accumulating garbage is shifting too fast, and we can't talk fast enough to keep up with our brain. And even if we could, others are limited in their willingness to drop their own garbage-sorting-balancing very often and listen to us.

Yet it's a real comfort when others try to hear what's behind our decisions. And it's especially comforting when they don't offer "help" and overload the shifting mass of garbage we're straining to sort out.

To me, what I believe keeps us from returning to our old lifestyle is gaining **firsthand** experience of the complexity and riskiness of **just keeping our own balance.**

It's this awareness which creates genuine compassion and appreciation for every other human being. And it's this same compassion and appreciation which makes it possible to feel the good feelings which come from listening deeply to each other... and responding deeply.

From this point on, everything we do, including the risk-taking we feared so much, is less hazardous. We're not alone and stuck, repeatedly asking, "What's the matter with me?" Instead, we're moving, living, and with eyes wide open. And it's exciting.   ☐

BIBLIOGRAPHY

Adams, David, The Role of Anger in the Consciousness Development of Peace Activists: Where Psychology and History Intersect, *International Journal of Psychophysiology* 4, 157-164. 1986

Allman, W.F., A Laboratory of Human Conflict, *U.S. News & World Report*, April 11, 1988.

Beck, Aaron T., *Cognitive Therapy and the Emotional Disorder*. New York: International Universities Press, 1976.

Burns, David, *Feeling Good*, New York: Basic Books (Harper Colophon), 1973

Chesney, Margaret A., Roseman, Ray H., (Eds.), *Anger and Hostility in Cardiovascular and Behavioral Disorders*. Washington, D.C.: Hemisphere Publishing Corporation, 1985.

   Chesney, Margaret A., Anger and Hostility: Future Implications for Behavioral Medicine.

   Durel, Lynn A. and Krantz, David, The Possible Effects of Beta-Adrenergic Blocking Drugs on Behavioral and Psychological Concomitants of Anger.

   Gentry, W. Doyle, Relationship of Anger-Coping Styles and Blood Pressure among Black Americans.

   Hecker, Michael H.L. and Lunde, Donald T., On the Diagnosis and Treatment of Chronically Hostile Individuals.

   Julius, Stevo, Schneider, Robert and Egan, Brent, Suppressed Anger in Hypertension: Facts and Problems.

   Manuck, Stephen B., Kaplan, Jay R., and Clarkson, Thomas B., An Animal Model of Coronary-Prone Behavior.

   Megaree, Edwin I., The Dynamics of Aggression and Their Application to Cardiovascular Disorders.

BIBLIOGRAPHY

Navaco, Raymond W., Anger and Its Therapeutic Relation.

Patterson, G.R., A Microsocial Analysis of Anger and Irritable Behavior.

Reid, John B. and Kavanagh, Kate A Social Interactional Approach to Child Abuse: Risk, Prevention and Treatment.

Rosenman, Ray H., Health Consequences of Anger and Implications for Treatment.

Siegel, Judith M., The Measurement of Anger as a Multidimensional Construct.

Spielberger, Charles D., Johnson, Ernest H. Russell, Stephen F., Crane, Rosario J., Jacobs, Gerard A., and Worden, Timothy J., The Experience and Expression of Anger: Construction and Validation of an Anger Expression Scale.

Williams, Jr., Redford B., Barefoot, John C., and Shekelle, Richard B., The Health Consequences of Hostility.

Cottington, Eric M., Matthews, Karen A., Talbott, Evelyn, and Kuller, Lewis H., Occupational Stress, Suppressed Anger and Hypertension, *Psychosomatic Medicine*, Vol. 48, No. 3/4. 1986.

Deffenbacher, Jerry L., Demm, P.M. and Brandon, Allen D., High General Anger: Correlates and Treatment. *Beh. Res. Ther.*, Vol. 24 #4, 481-489, 1986.

Dimsdale, Joel E., Pierce, Chester, Schoenfeld, David, Brown, Anne, Zusman, Randall, and Graham, Robert. Suppressed Anger and Blood Pressure: The Effects of Race, Sex, Social Class, Obesity and Age. *Psychosomatic Medicine*, Vol. 49, No. 6, 1986.

Ellis, Albert, *How to Live with and without Anger*, New York: Reader's Digest Press, 1977.

_____, *A Guide to Rational Living*. North Hollywood, Calif.: Wilshire Books, 1961.

BIBLIOGRAPHY

Hassebrauck, Manfred, Ragings of Distress as a Function of Degree and Kind of Inequity, *The Journal of Social Psychology,* 126 (2), 268-270, 1986.

Hazaleus, Susan L. and Deffenbacher, Jerry L., Relaxation and Cognitive Treatment of Anger. *Journal of Consulting and Clinical Psychology*, Vol. 54, No. 2, 222-226, 1986.

Julius, Mara, Harburg, Ernest, Cottington, Eric M. and Johnson, Ernest H., Anger-coping Types, Blood Pressure, and All-cause Mortality: A follow-up in Tecumseh, Michigan (1971-1983). *American Journal of Epidemiology.* The John Hopkins University School of Hygiene and Public Health. 1986.

Kiley, Dan, *Wendy Dilemma.* New York, Prentice Hall Press, 1989.

Leaf, Russell C., Gross, Paget Hope, Todres, Amy K., Marcus, Susan, and Bradford, Barry. Placebo-like Effects of Education about Rational-Emotive Therapy, *Psychological Reports*, 58, 351-370, 1986.

Lerner, Harriett Goldhor, *The Dance of Anger.* New York: Harper and Row, 1985.

McKay, Matthew, Rogers, Peter D., McKay, Judith, *When Anger Hurts.* Oakland, Calif.: New Harbinger Publications, Inc. 1989.

Miller, Annetta, Springer, Karen, Gordon, Jeanne, Murr, Andrew, Cohn, Bob, Drew, Lisa, and Barrett, Todd. Stress on the Job, *Newsweek*, 40-48, April 25, 1988.

Nelson, Jane, *Positive Discipline*, Fair Oaks, Calif. Sunrise Press, 1981.

Norwood, Robin, *Women Who Love Too Much*, New York. Pocket Books, a Division of Simon and Schuster. 1986.

Oliver, Carol H. and Schneider, Eric, Communication Awareness: Rx for Angry Patients, *American Pharmacy*, Vol. NS26, No. 3, 93-94, March 1986-249.

BIBLIOGRAPHY

Rubin, Theodore I., *The Angry Book,* New York: McMillan Publishing Co. 1969.

Schneider, Robert H., Egan, Brent M., Johnson, Ernest H., Drobny, Herman, and Herman, and Julius, Stevo, Anger and Anxiety in Borderline Hypertension. New York, *Psychomatic Medicine*, Vol. 48, No. 3/4 (March/April) 1986.

Siegel, Judith M., The Multidimensional Anger Inventory. *Journal of Personality and Social Psychology,* Vol. 51, No. 1, 191-200. 1986.

Sonkin, Daniel Jay and Durphy, Michael, *Learning to Live Without Violence*. San Francisco: Volcano Publishing Co. 1985.

Tavris, Carol. *Anger, the Misunderstood Emotion*, New York: Simon and Schuster, 1982.

Weisinger, Hendrie. *Dr. Weisinger's Anger Work Out Book*, New York: Quill, 1985.

INDEX

anger, a habit to replace it,   70

anger, a knife to the heart,   100, 108, 128

anger as a motivator,   114, 168

anger, getting it out,   111-114, 144, 168

anger habit,   69

ANGER PUZZLE, THE,   125, 169

BREAK THE ANGER TRAP,   169

detectives,   72

jealousy,   129-131

marriage insurance,   177

monologues and long notes,   165, 166

murder,   80

over-reach/fall-back,   55

Portuguese saying,   166

questions as communication blocks,   166-167

Rooney, Pat,   98, 125, 164, 169, 170

SHAKE THE ANGER HABIT!,   98, 118, 125, 145, 169

suicide,   64, 80, 107, 153, 174

ORDER FORM   THE BOOKERY PUBLISHING CO.

6899 Riata Dr. Redding, CA 96002   (916) 365 8068 FAX (916) 365 8082

❖Order by phone, FAX or mail. Full refund if not satisfied❖

____ GETTING THROUGH TO OTHERS WITHOUT ANGER $ _____
(1993 Doty) ISBN 0-930822-17-X, $11.95

____ SHAKE THE ANGER HABIT! (1990, Doty/Rooney) $ _____
ISBN 0-930822-10-2, $11.95

____ Audio cassette SHAKE THE ANGER HABIT! $ _____
 ISBN 0-930822-12-9, $24.95

____ THE ANGER PUZZLE (1986, Doty/Rooney) $ _____
ISBN 0-930822-07-2, $8.95

____ BREAK THE ANGER TRAP (1985, Doty) $ _____
ISBN 0-930822-06-4, $8.95

____ MARRIAGE INSURANCE (1978, Doty) $ _____
ISBN 0-930822-01-3 (a series of communication exercises
for two people to use together), $8.95

■ To hear the author on a local talkshow, ask the station to contact
the Bookery, or we'll make the contact if you provide the address and
phone number. Ask about the forthcoming book,
100 THINGS WE CAN DO ABOUT ANGER AND VIOLENCE.

■ The first two books listed below (both hardbound and handbound)
show how using copy machine printing and handbinding make it
possible to create multiple copies of our own books (one more way
of trying to get through to others).

____ HEY LOOK . . . I MADE A BOOK ! $ _____
(1992, Doty/Meredith) ISBN 0-930822-15-3 $12.95

____ PUBLISH YOUR OWN HANDBOUND BOOKS $ _____
(1980, Doty), comes with materials for making a blank book-
order by mail only, $12.95.

____ Materials packet for making a blank book $ _____
4 1/4" x 5 3/4"- order by mail only, $4.50

____ THE SELF-PUBLISHING MANUAL (1993, Dan
Poynter) ISBN 0-915516-66-7, $19.95 $ _____

Ship to: Subtotal $ _____

_____   Calif. Sales Tax $ _____

_____   Shipping flat rate $ _2.00_

_____(any number of items)

_____   TOTAL ENCLOSED$ _____

214